Shine

Brought to you by Swansea University students

Published in 2025 by Discover Your Bounce Publishing
www.discoveryourbouncepublishing.com
Copyright © Discover Your Bounce Publishing
All rights reserved.
Printed in the United States of America & the UK. No part of this book may be used, replicated or reproduced, stored in a retrieval system, or transmitted in any form or by any means, electronic, mechanical, photocopying, recording, or otherwise, without the written permission of the author(s). Quotations of no more than 25 words are permitted, but only if used solely for the purposes of critical articles or reviews.

ISBN: 978-1-914428-39-5

Although the author and publisher have made every effort to ensure that the information in this book is correct at the time of going to print, the author and publisher do not assume and therefore disclaim liability to any party. The author and the publisher will not be held responsible for any loss or damage save for that caused by their negligence.

Although the author and the publisher have made every reasonable attempt to achieve accuracy in the content of this book, they assume no responsibility for errors or omissions.

Page design and typesetting by Discover Your Bounce Publishing

CONTENTS

Foreword	i
About Swansea University	iii
A Note from Our Partners	iv
Dedication	vi
Brandon Havard - Wasting Valuable Time or Life's Most Valuable Lessons?	1
C.A. - Finding Me	7
C.B. - Against All Odds: A Tale of University Life and Personal Growth	12
Corey Connor - My Route to Prosperity	18
Edna Jeo - Embracing Uncertainty: My Journey to Finding the Right Path	23
Emilia Rucinska - Spicy Brain	29
Fahad Mohammad - Opening Doors Through Language	35
Faith Adebisi – Just Have Faith	41
Gemma Rees - Smelling of Roses	47
I.O. - The Journey Before the Destination	53
James Thomas-Wood - Grey Scrubs – Bright Purpose	59
Kat Adamczyk-Rees - From Misfit to Success	65
Lewys Tectonic - I Can't Have it All (I'm Still Gonna Try)	71

Shine

Lily Carline - Every Twist and Turn	77
Mia Bergin - Everyone Moves at Their Own Pace (And That's Okay)	83
Oluwatosin Alatise - Lots of Lucky Little Detours	88
Sarah Howell - Follow Your Dreams	94
Siân Gibson - Dreams vs Reality	100
Tirzah Velauthapillai - Breaking Barriers: A Tamil Girl's Journey to the Stars	106
Therese Elnar - Through the Loops: Resilience in the Face of Life's Rollercoaster	112
Willow Browning - Crohn's University and Me	118
Yasmin Santiago - Invest in Yourself	124
About T.G. Consulting	130
University Resources and Information	132
Helpful Organisations	135

Foreword

At Swansea University, we believe in the power of opportunity - an environment where ambition meets action, and potential turns into achievement. From our breathtaking campuses on the stunning Welsh coastline to the vibrant, inclusive community within, Swansea is a place where students don't just learn - they thrive.

Central to this ethos is **Career Boost**, a groundbreaking programme funded by MEDR and crafted to empower students from underrepresented backgrounds. Career Boost is more than a support system - it's a launchpad. With access to bespoke work placements, employability bursaries, personalised career coaching, and dedicated mentors, students are equipped to overcome barriers, take control of their futures, and redefine what success means to them.

The stories in this book shine a spotlight on the remarkable journeys of students who've embraced Career Boost to transform their prospects. Whether they've gained invaluable experience, unlocked new opportunities, or built networks that will shape their careers, these

Shine

individuals exemplify resilience, creativity, and the courage to dream big.

As you turn these pages, you'll not only celebrate the achievements of these incredible students but also glimpse the vibrant possibilities that Swansea University offers. It's a place where innovation thrives, challenges are embraced, and futures are built. Welcome to Swansea University - a place where your story begins, and the possibilities are limitless.

Lucy Griffiths
Head of Careers, Employability and Placements
Swansea University

Shine

About Swansea University

Since 1920, Swansea University has been at the forefront of world-class research and education, growing into a globally connected institution where innovation and societal impact thrive. Over the past century, we have built a legacy of groundbreaking research and a commitment to improving lives through education, collaboration, and enterprise.

Our work spans every aspect of life - from advancing health and well-being to fostering cultural growth and addressing global challenges such as climate change and sustainability. This commitment extends to our students, who are encouraged to actively participate in research and innovation that makes a real difference in communities around the world.

Deeply rooted in Swansea Bay, we are proud to serve as the region's university while building connections that reach far beyond Wales. Our vibrant and inclusive community provides students with the tools to think critically, adapt to a changing world, and thrive in their personal and professional lives.

Collaboration and enterprise are integral to Swansea University's ethos. Founded in partnership with industry, we continue to work with local and global organisations to drive innovation, create opportunities, and tackle the big issues of our time. As we move forward, our focus remains on inspiring future generations, improving lives, and shaping a more sustainable, equitable world.

A Note from Our Partners

Every person carries within them a story of experiences, challenges, triumphs, and moments of growth that shape who they are. This book is a celebration of those stories. It is a collection of lived experiences shared by students who, are navigating their unique journeys through life. Every person featured in this book has walked a unique path, overcoming challenges, discovering passions, and building connections that shaped who they are today.

In these pages, you will find reflections of resilience, vulnerability, and the incredible strength that comes from embracing one's authentic self. These stories are not just words on a page, they are windows into the hearts and minds of individuals who have dared to share their truths, to inspire, and to remind us all of the power of community and understanding. Through these pages, you will find inspiration, strength, and a reminder that your own experiences, whether joyful, challenging, or transformative, are valuable. You are the author of your story, and your voice matters.

Shine

As you read, may you see your own experiences mirrored in these narratives and recognise the beauty of your own story. May you feel encouraged to embrace the lessons life has to offer and to share your voice with the world, knowing that it is valuable, meaningful, and needed.

This book is a reminder that through every challenge and triumph, we are never alone.

We invite you to read with an open heart, to reflect, and perhaps even to find a piece of yourself in these pages.

As partners in this project, we are proud of the diversity and resilience reflected here. Our goal is to support you as you navigate your own path, learn from others, and build a future that reflects your dreams.

Maria Esposito

Head of Partnerships, TG Consulting Ltd

Dedication

This book is dedicated to every individual who despite facing challenges on their journey continue to *shine* through adversity. We hope you will resonate with the experiences shared within this book and find inspiration to implement into your own journey.

Wasting Valuable Time or Life's Most Valuable Lessons?
By Brandon Havard

Life happens when you're busy making other plans. Sitting here now at the ripe old age of twenty-eight, I have come to the realisation that John Lennon was right when he said that 'Life is what happens to you when you're busy making other plans.' You see, the harder you try to control your life, the more it controls you; we spend so much of our time worrying about where we are heading in life that we miss the real-life things that happen every day.

Having exhausted many avenues and needlessly stumbling down some ponderous dead ends, I have spent a good portion of my youth wasting what I thought was valuable time. I have made mistakes in my life, and though I still find myself making wrong decisions, they do not seem foolish or wrong at the time. Something I've learned on my journey so far is that through our mistakes we learn some of life's best and most valuable lessons, so much so that I have learned to value the mistakes I have made, as I know now that what I thought was wasted time was not wasted time at all. Every decision I have ever made, each bump and wrong turn, the good and the bad, has led me to where I am today.

Where it all began. While most University experiences tend to last three to five years, my experience with university has been a little different. My journey began around eight years ago, when I decided to enroll at UWE Bristol. Having dropped out of sixth form at the end of year twelve and spending a couple of years trying my hand at things, I discovered a niche job that few people had heard of which offered a decent salary; quantity surveying. What is quantity surveying, you ask? Well, it's the rather mundane job of quantifying construction projects. To be completely honest, I never really wanted to be a surveyor of any kind, but to me, it sounded cool, and I probably liked the reaction it got from people more than the job itself. You see, a lot of what I did during these years was not for myself, not at all. Between the ages of fifteen and twenty-two, I had no clue of what direction I was heading and so found myself doing the things that my friends were doing. Now, with the power of hindsight, I know that I had no intentions of becoming a quantity surveyor. Instead, I was merely using the opportunity to move away from home and desperately try and preserve the endless possibilities of childhood.

For years, I had spent so much of my childhood wanting to be so many different things that I never truly settled on what it was I wanted to do. From a young age, I enjoyed basking in the endless possibilities childhood provided me with. Would I become a police officer? A civil engineer? An astronaut? I didn't know, nor did I mind, as long as I had the time to wonder about what the future might bring. Whereas many of my friends and those around me knew exactly what path they'd be taking and worked tirelessly to achieve their aspirations, it was mind-boggling to me why my peers spent so much time revising and studying. I could never understand why people would get stressed out over their GCSEs; I thought that life would just work out ok. For a while, my attitude towards a career was manageable whilst I had friends in the same boat. But sure enough, one by one, they embarked on their post-school journeys until only I was left. Looking back, this is where I began to panic and throw myself at anything and everything. This void-filling, as I call it, led me to chase the things I had little to no interest in. I was left doing things that made it look like I was heading somewhere, but in reality, I found myself with no direction and accelerating down the path of no return.

Bridge over troubled waters. After a year or two trying my hand at things, I stumbled upon quantity surveying and so began mapping out a way to achieve what was to be a short-lived goal. Having spent a year in college achieving the qualifications I didn't achieve in sixth form; I was on my way to university for the first time. However, I had no intentions of becoming a quantity surveyor, and my time in Bristol could be summed up as further void-filling. But my time in Bristol was not a failure, far from it, I gained valuable life experience that will stay with me forever. I started my own band, played in some of the best venues in Bristol, and featured on BBC Radio. I made friends and memories, but most importantly, I met a girl. On my first day in Bristol, I met Freya, my now wife-to-be and mother of my children. That was the day my life changed.

Having spent the following few years in Bristol, when my partner became pregnant, we moved back to Wales. It was during this time that I began to think seriously about my life. Who was I? What did I love to do? It was after the birth of our first born that I really felt the need to better myself, to strive and become the best version of myself that was possible. I had struggled for so long not knowing what I wanted that it suddenly dawned on me, much of the struggle was because I never factored in what I actually wanted for myself.

Having always had a love for history and an ever-growing interest in politics and academia, I began yet again mapping out a way to achieve my goal. This is where we come to Swansea University.

Swansea, Oh Swansea! While I had shopped around, so to speak, for suitable universities and courses, Swansea University was a no-brainer for many reasons. Not only is Swansea my local university, but it also boasts a range of world-leading academics, many of whom have really helped me build my confidence in an academic setting. At first, going back to university felt a bit odd; being a mature student and a father I was sceptical about how I would connect with others and whether I would make any acquaintances. Nevertheless, I was amazed to find out that the university had a social hour once a month for mature students and commuters which was something that I benefited from in my first few months. Settling into the university was a breeze; meeting other mature students and the easy way in which we were introduced to our subjects and lecturers during first year, was great. I cannot express enough gratitude for some of my lecturers during my time at Swansea, not only are they helpful and teach to a high standard, but they are ultra-supportive and are always there for a friendly chat.

Perhaps the biggest factor that made Swansea the no-brainer choice for me, however, was the opportunity to intern at the Welsh Parliament during my third year. As someone aspiring for a career in Welsh politics, such an opportunity was like a dream come true for me. The internship was part of a double-term module that is undertaken instead of a dissertation. This, along with the fact that I was able to study some of my modules in Welsh, made Swansea University my one and only choice. As part of the Senedd Module, I was given the opportunity to intern for Sioned Williams, my local Member of the Senedd. For this module, I had to write a policy report based on the issues I worked on during my internship, which contains recommendations to the Welsh Government concerning the issue of child poverty. The opportunity to work in the Senedd was such a surreal experience, from watching Rhun ap Iorwerth on ITV during the General Election to working in the same office was just awesome. My time in the Senedd also opened many doors that would have otherwise remained unopened. For example, I recently stood as the Plaid Cymru candidate in a County Council by-election, in which I came second by only 43 votes, and am also now the Secretary for the Cwmtawe branch of Plaid Cymru. Both of these opportunities were the direct result of my internship, for which I will forever be grateful to the University and Professor Bradbury for providing such an invaluable stepping stone in my career development.

Shine

Throughout my time at Swansea University, it is safe to say that I have gained experiences that will be crucial for my career development, and I have made connections that I will cherish for the rest of my life. Through the 'Employability Zone', I was not only given the amazing opportunity to share my story but have also been given the chance to work on the Richard Burton Centenary Project alongside the Richard Burton Archives at the university. Furthermore, I was also fortunate enough to be an editor of the politics department's student led academic journal 'Populo', a role I am very proud of.

It would be no exaggeration to say that Swansea University has changed my life and has done a great job at setting me up for the future, for which I will forever be grateful.

Finding Me
By C.A.

In the Igbo culture, birth order and gender greatly shape a child's role in the family. The Ada, the first daughter of the family, carries a weighty responsibility recognised as a pillar of honor and dedication. As the Ada in my family, I have carried the mantle of responsibility and expectation, shaping my identity long before I understood who I truly was and what I wanted from life. I lived in constant tension between an immense pressure to succeed and an ever-present fear of failure. I was stuck, paralysed between what I should be doing and the fear of not knowing what I wanted to do. I existed as a concept—someone for my siblings to aspire to, something for my parents to brag about. But where was me? Where did I fit into all of this?

I was the easy child. Don't get me wrong, I talked a lot and was bossy, but I didn't make things harder. From a young age, I wanted to be someone my parents could be proud of, so initially, I dreamed of being a lawyer like my grandpa, who died when I was a baby but lived through my father's stories. A great lawyer whom my father missed dearly, and I guess I felt a need to fill this gap and to 'be something' for my parents. I always had this innate sense that there were lines I shouldn't cross. It made life easier for my parents, who were raised alongside me, and I found safety within the lines. My siblings, bolder and more confident, grew outside those boundaries. I often resented them for that. It is only now I realise—what sacrifice did I expect them to make? They were simply children, something I rarely allowed myself to be.

Shine

My family moved constantly. We joked that for every move, we had to get a lifelong souvenir. Four countries, four children. My father's medical career dictated our lives, and with every achievement, we were on the move. With each move, I felt I left a part of me behind. I still feel fragmented; parts of me that should have combined to make a person, split off and didn't fully form enough to integrate. I knew who I was supposed to be, and for a while, that felt enough, but really, looking back it wasn't. In high school, I worked towards dreams of working as a doctor, but my concept of self made no sense beyond **shoulds and musts**. That was a common theme throughout my adolescence—**what I should be doing?** I was paralysed as a teenager, feeling overwhelmed by expectations.

Twelve-year-old me thought everything was so straightforward. If I did what I was supposed to, everything would fall into place. By my senior year, burnout consumed me. Years of endless, tireless ambition, and yet I still faced rejection. My senior year is a blur of sleeping, skipping classes, and keeping up the good daughter facade. Outside of my academics, outside of being the 'easy' child, outside of who I was supposed to be, there was nothing.

I felt empty. I enrolled at a respected local university, and my life felt decided. I would stay local. Everyone was so proud of me, but it didn't feel right. Then fate intervened. The idea of Clearing came up through some family friends. As I began researching Clearing for hopeful medical students, Swansea's medical pathway appeared. I'll admit I ignored it. Wales?! What business did I have there? I told myself for the first time I'd be staying local, not going somewhere new, but Swansea kept popping up, and I couldn't help but be interested. This is where my perspective on what I should be doing began to shift. When August 21st hit— three phones at the ready—Swansea gave me a place.

My decision wasn't completely supported. My mom hesitated, my dad was cautiously supportive, and I only told my friends days before I left. For the first time, this was completely and truly me. I did feel guilty. I felt like I was abandoning something. Perhaps it was the Ada in me telling me not to go anywhere. But for once in my life, there wasn't any expectation. I truly had no idea what to expect. Maybe I'd regret it, but this was completely my decision to regret. And just like that, something *clicked*.

"Do you have ADHD?"

My new roommate asked this within an hour of our first interaction. I was taken aback—not entirely surprised, though. Earlier that year, my father had suggested I get evaluated. Due to my own indignation, I was not tested. If I'm honest, I did think I had it, but to me, I saw the diagnosis of neurodivergence as officially admitting that something was a little off with me. I was used to being the helper, the problem solver; not the one who needed help.

But alone in the UK, finding my footing and being outside of my comfort zone exposed a lot of my symptoms that I usually carefully masked. I struggled the first two years in Swansea. I was inattentive, disorganised, and so emotional. I was falling behind and feeling so lost. It wasn't until I found my people - the Aerial Club - that my perspective on neurodivergence began to change. The Aerial Club housed the first group of people who understood me and encouraged me to finally get the help I needed. I started seeing a psychologist and trying medication. I was able to get my life on track. I was less distracted, less emotionally volatile. The world was quieter, and my future didn't seem so daunting. Through therapy, I worked on the internal stigmas I had toward myself and my condition. With support from the university's disabilities department, I finally found stability. I felt like I could breathe for the first time academically. The newfound clarity pushed me beyond survival mode and encouraged me to take more opportunities in school, so I joined the Student Ambassador Scheme.

My work as a Student Ambassador was more than another extracurricular activity, it was a turning point in my perspective on what success means. It gave me the chance to help others navigate their own journeys. I found myself giving advice to prospective students, sharing my own experience of uncertainty, and I realised things I once viewed as weaknesses - my ADHD, my unusual path, and my obstacles - were strengths, giving me empathy, perspective, and the ability to connect with students facing similar doubts.

As a Career Ambassador, I took this role even further, engaging with my department in ways I hadn't anticipated, working with faculty, gaining shadowing opportunities, and reshaping my approach toward my future. I refined my CV, learned how to present myself not only as a student but as a professional. Through workshops, interview prep, and career consultations, I stopped seeing success as a rigid path with a single destination but rather as something I can build, piece by piece, through the opportunities I seek out and the work I put in.

For the first time, I wasn't following a path or doing what I was supposed to do—I was actively shaping my life.

Swansea University changed more than my academic trajectory; it helped shape my meaning of success. It reignited my passion for my chosen field—not just as an expectation to fulfill but as a career I could truly make my own. Working with my department, seeking mentorship, and embracing opportunities like academic shadowing, I've realised medicine isn't just something I should do; it is what I want to do. More importantly, Swansea gave me the space to discover myself beyond expectations. It allowed me to step outside the role of the 'perfect' Ada and into the role of someone still learning, growing, and figuring things out. My worth isn't in the expectations I meet but in the person I am becoming.

I'm still figuring out who I am, but for the first time, I am moving forward because I want to.

Finding me will be the most important thing I do.

And I'm happy to do it.

Against All Odds: A Tale of University Life and Personal Growth
By C.B.

As a 20-year-old attending university, my path here has been anything but straightforward. My journey has been marked by challenges that have shaped my resilience and drive to succeed. Despite facing loneliness, loss and instability, I am determined to show that no matter your background, it is possible to rise and achieve your goals.

In secondary school and sixth form, I was often on the fringes, watching others form friendships that seemed effortless. While I longed to connect, I hesitated, fearing rejection and growing used to solitude. This habit of staying in the background followed me to university, where social circles formed quickly. Although I wanted to be part of them, the comfort of solitude was hard to shake. I retreated into my studies and daily routines, often feeling like an outsider. The barrier between me and others was built over years of isolation and loss.

Growing up, my family was anything but stable. People often assumed we were well-off, but behind closed doors, my family struggled financially, moving frequently, dealing with the loss of my father. My father passed away when I was 12. Our relationship had been strained and distant. His passing didn't hit me with the grief one might expect but left a complex void – one that did not inspire deep sadness but a sense of detachment. I learned to bury feelings and a put on a facade of normalcy to the outside world.

University represented a new chapter, a place where I hoped to redefine myself and break free from past insecurities. Yet, the same patterns of isolation followed me, and I initially struggled to build connections. However, my studies quickly became a source of motivation and purpose. I found the university environment supportive and inspiring, providing both academic growth and opportunities to connect with peers and mentors who shared my interests.

Determined to push myself, I started joining study groups and attending my course's society events. My early attempts to socialise were uncomfortable, often reinforcing my insecurities, but the connections I made were worth the effort. I began forming friendships and, for the first time, I felt seen and understood. Slowly, I started to find my place and build a sense of belonging that I had always craved. The people I met became my support system, giving me the confidence to step out of my comfort zone.

I discovered my passion for genetics during my first year. I had initially chosen this field because it seemed intellectually stimulating, but a specific course module on genetic disorders resonated deeply. Understanding the science behind hereditary conditions and the potential for medical intervention sparked a desire to use my studies in ways that could directly help others. That realisation was powerful, as I saw my own academic journey aligning with a career path that felt both challenging and rewarding.

The journey has not been without its challenges. Balancing academic responsibilities, personal life, and the weight of my past was often overwhelming. I used to feel that handling everything on my own was a sign of strength, but during a particularly difficult period, I reached out to the university's anonymous counselling services. Talking to someone about my feelings was a humbling experience, but it was also the beginning of true healing. The service helped me unpack years of buried emotions, showing me that seeking help was not a weakness but a necessary step in growth.

Counselling helped me develop coping mechanisms and strategies that I could apply to both my personal life and studies. Techniques like mindfulness, journaling, and setting boundaries became part of my routine, allowing me to manage stress and prioritise my mental health. These practices taught me the importance of caring for myself and gave me tools to handle setbacks with resilience. I grew more confident in my ability to face challenges and found resilience I hadn't realised I possessed. As I began to focus more on my well-being, I also saw a positive shift, helping me to feel more grounded and in control.

Throughout my journey, I have been fortunate to find people who have guided and inspired me. One professor in particular played a significant role in shaping my career goals. His dedication to research and his commitment to helping students succeed reminded me that academia could be a powerful space for growth and innovation. His encouragement motivated me to pursue research opportunities and explored my course field more deeply.

Although I have not yet had the opportunity to participate in research, this professor's guidance has sparked my curiosity and strengthened my resolve to seek out such experiences in the future. He often shared insights about his own research journey, discussing the challenges and rewards of investigating complex questions. These conversations inspired me to think critically about the issues within my field and how I might contribute to addressing them. His mentorship also encouraged me to develop skills that will be essential when I do engage in research. For example, I have improved on my ability to analyse information, communicate effectively, and approach problems with creativity. These skills, coupled with his encouragement, have given me the confidence to pursue opportunities such as internships or academic programs that offer a research component.

Looking forward, my career goals are clear: I aspire to work in both genetics and medicine, focusing on research that can lead to life-changing discoveries. I plan to further my studies and gain practical experience through research projects and placement opportunities in hospitals, where I can apply what I've learned to real-world challenges. My academic journey at Swansea has shown me that each step I take brings me closer to making a meaningful impact in my field and in the lives of others.

Over time, my perspective on my career has evolved. What began as a general interest has transformed into a mission to help others by using the scientific knowledge I gain to contribute to healthcare solutions. I now understand that my past challenges have equipped me with unique insights and resilience that will benefit my career. Rather than seeing adversity as a setback, I view it as a source of strength that will guide me in my professional journey. My story has become more than just my own; it is now part of my purpose to create positive change in the lives of others.

Shine

For students just beginning their journey, I would advise them to embrace challenges as opportunities for growth. University is a unique time to explore new areas and push beyond comfort zones. Seeking support—whether through lecturers, friends, or family—is invaluable; don't hesitate to reach out when things feel overwhelming. Remember, resilience isn't about never struggling; it's about finding the courage to keep moving forward, even when obstacles seem insurmountable. Growth often happens in the most unexpected ways and moments, especially when we learn to lean on others as well as ourselves.

Looking back, I see how every challenge has shaped my resilience and clarity of purpose. We all carry burdens—some visible, some hidden—but it is how we confront them that defines our path. I have learned that true strength comes from within and that it is possible to transform adversity into opportunity. The challenges I faced have shaped me into who I am today, instilling in me a sense of determination and perseverance that will carry me forward in life.

As I move forward, I am committed to using my journey as a foundation for a future that I once only dreamed of. The lessons I've learned at Swansea and the experiences I've had here have not only equipped me with academic skills but have also given me the courage to pursue a career in a field that can truly make a difference. My story is a testament to the fact that no matter where you come from or the obstacles you face, you can rise above and create a life of purpose and meaning.

At Swansea, I discovered the power of resilience and the importance of embracing challenges as opportunities for growth. The supportive environment fostered by faculty and peers helped me unlock potential I didn't know I had. Whether it was through engaging lectures, collaborative projects, or moments of personal reflection, every experience has shaped me into a more confident and determined individual.

As I look ahead, I am eager to channel this growth into making a tangible impact. I am driven by a desire to contribute to my community, uplift others, and continue learning throughout my life. Swansea has taught me that success is not only about personal achievement but also about empowering others to succeed. I am excited to carry these lessons with me as I strive to create a meaningful, impactful career that reflects the values and aspirations nurtured during my time here.

My Route to Prosperity
By Corey Connor

The journey of self-growth isn't always the easiest path. My route to prosperity, a word I love to live by, has been a tumultuous one. It has been a highly emotional rollercoaster that has led me to who I am today.

Life back home has never been simple. I grew up in a household with not much money at all, but in fairness to my parents, they did everything they could to ensure that I had the best possible platform that they could provide to succeed. Sure, I wasn't turning up to school with brand new coats, shoes, equipment like the rest of the other children, but I really couldn't have cared less as the efforts of both my parents to make sure I had everything I needed was absolutely incredible. What they lacked in finances, they made up for and more in the love and care they provided me with.

My mother has always been a woman with an absolute heart of gold. She is unique, and I don't believe there is a single soul similar to her. She has had to deal with consistent heart issues from birth, with doctors continually setting new life expectancies that she continues to outlive. She is an absolute inspiration to anyone who ever gets to know her story. My mum has always had ill-health; every Christmas she would spend about 4-6 weeks extremely ill, which was always a kicker because of how much she loves Christmas. Her ill health would often continue throughout the year. At some points it coupled up with my grandfather becoming extremely ill too. Despite having to help look after her over the years, my mother and I have always got on with each other and we have had a bond more respective of best friends than the typical mother and son dynamic. This bond was quite a stark difference with my dad.

My dad has always been an extremely caring, selfless, loving father, but his traumatising childhood always reared its ugly head whenever we would have even the slightest difference in opinion. My father was never physically threatening as a child, but his temper would spiral very quickly, and very intensely. I was a joker as a child, I loved to wind up everyone about everything, something I developed from my grandfather. I still am a joker now, but when I was younger, my dad took it more as disrespectful rather than the playfulness it was intended as. This led to a rather serious strain in our relationship. I started to become disrespectful because I felt that as I was going to be accused of it, I may as well start to act it, right? Despite this strain in our relationship, my father tirelessly looked after the family, caring for my mother, while working night shifts and trying to achieve a degree, which he got with second class honours, to provide more for our family.

Now, I couldn't be prouder of my parents. They have always helped to provide for me despite the setbacks in their own lives. They are young parents, so we, in a way, grew up together. As they were learning about their own lives, they were trying to help guide me through mine, and for that I genuinely could not be more grateful. The person I am today has been heavily influenced by the kindness and compassion that my parents showed to everyone around them.

Shine

The way my parents brought me up prepared me tremendously for my time in Swansea University; it helped me to come straight into a new experience with open-mindedness. As a result of growing up the way I did, with the support my parents gave, I found it relatively easy to transfer my previous educational and life experiences into this newfound world of education and freedom. I lived on my own, in a city relatively new to me, studying for one of the hardest degrees you can study for – accounting and finance. Now, university hasn't been a walk in the park, I have gone above expectations with some modules, fallen short in others, but overall I have done really well, both in university and out. This experience has helped me to develop as a professional, whilst continuing the personal development I had already started as a result of my childhood.

University is different to any other experience; for the first time for most, you are all alone, miles away from familiarity and tasked with studying some of the most difficult to understand texts in your chosen degree field. I chose to study accounting and finance. I chose this topic as it represents years of what I found came naturally to me in school: business and mathematics. In my opinion, accounting and finance best represents them both, meaning that I would not only be able to do well, but as I enjoyed business studies and mathematics before, I would love to be able to work in an environment where the two were virtually one and the same. Studying in Swansea would prove to be a brilliant decision, as it has helped me to shape my career path to what it is now.

Over my time in Swansea University, I have attended multiple careers events and have had the privilege to complete an internship as a HR

Shine

Intern at a local not-for-profit housing association. This was my first ever corporate role, shaping me as a professional. Whilst HR wasn't always my biggest priority, nor what I ultimately wanted to work as – I want to work in finance or accounting long-term – the experience still allowed me to get a taste for corporate work. I was even lucky enough to sit in with the finance department to get a brief understanding of how my education with Swansea University would be put into practice.

During my third year in Swansea, I was lucky enough to be offered the opportunity to complete a year in industry. I worked for a local timber importer, where I was able to experience business operations, corporate finance, and measures of accounting for small businesses first-hand. Working there was a key element in my educational journey with Swansea University to become a professional in the workplace. I was able to demonstrate knowledge gained from university along with my personality which developed through my upbringing. In my placement I utilised all these steps of my development, both as a professional and as a person. I have finished the placement now and due to the strides I have made through this professional experience, I feel that I managed to make the year in industry absolutely and entirely successful.

My personal experiences with growing up has ultimately shaped my career aspirations. I have always wanted to give back or work in family-owned businesses. For example, I chose the internship with the non-profit housing association because it gave me the opportunity to be able to help the vulnerable people that the association provided for. The internship was an important part of my professional education; providing me with a place to study and learn what actually happens in practice. My placement was integral to how I see business operations; I was given the opportunity to complete a wide variety of actions in the business. This gave me a well-rounded view of what it takes to do almost all aspects of practical business functions.

When I look at my professional journey so far, and my developing career path, I see that the person I am now, is far and away a much more mature and wiser individual than when I initially started in university. I have been mentored by my manager in my placement to become a more well-rounded employee, and an asset to anywhere I work in the future. This mentoring has driven me to be the person I am now.

My advice to students who are beginning their career journey, is don't get stuck in the mindset of only wanting to do one thing; be open minded! Try everything you can, take every opportunity, don't leave any stone unturned, and make sure that you never end up regretting not taking certain opportunities and paths. Everyone has a career end goal, but no pathway is ever the same, let your career run its course and see where you end up. Your professional journey is important, but it will never be as important as your journey of life itself. Let them play out, take as many opportunities as you can, and enjoy watching your personal life and professional life flourish!

Embracing Uncertainty: My Journey to Finding the Right Path
By Edna Jeo

Growing up, I never had a clear idea of what I wanted to do. While most of my peers seemed to have their futures meticulously planned out, I always felt like I was floating in a sea of uncertainty, desperately searching for something to anchor me. The advice I received was always the same; choose subjects you enjoy, and eventually, you'll find a profession that suits you. The problem? While I found certain subjects interesting, I never felt a deep passion for any one area. I studied diligently and enjoyed learning, but I struggled to pinpoint a subject that truly excited me. However, I did enjoy the sciences, except for physics, which I was not too keen on. So, when the time came to make decisions about my future, I naturally gravitated toward a career in the science industry. Medicine was never my cup of tea, but dentistry? That intrigued me. It seemed like a stable and respectable profession, one that combined science with hands-on skills, so I convinced myself it was the right choice.

Wanting to keep my options open, I chose biology and chemistry, knowing they were essential for dentistry. I also picked maths, reasoning that it would always be useful no matter which career path I eventually pursued. At the time, it felt like a strategic choice; a safety net in case I lost interest in dentistry along the way. And, as it turned out, that's exactly what happened. During my A-levels, I found myself growing increasingly frustrated with the sciences. What had once seemed like a reasonable and stable career path soon became something

I dreaded. I struggled to stay engaged and questioned whether I was truly cut out for this field. But by then, I had already put in so much effort: virtual work experiences, setting up a dentistry club, countless applications, and rigorous entrance tests. The thought of throwing it all away felt like failure. I told myself that I had invested too much to quit now. So, I kept pushing forward, convincing myself that I could make it work, even as a nagging doubt lingered in the back of my mind, growing stronger with each passing day.

But then, out of the blue, everything changed. By the end of my A-level journey, a routine visit to my dentist made me realise beyond any doubt that dentistry wasn't for me. Sitting in that chair, observing the environment, and picturing myself in that role for the rest of my life, I knew I couldn't do it. My heart sank. I wanted so badly to force myself to feel differently, to silence the growing certainty that I was on the wrong path. But I couldn't ignore it anymore. It was a moment of clarity unlike any I had experienced before. And then, just as quickly as the panic had set in, something else followed. It was a wave of relief so intense it was almost overwhelming. I felt lighter, as if a huge weight had been lifted off my shoulders. I knew I needed to move in a different direction. For the first time in a long time, I allowed myself to consider a different path, one that felt like a better fit. Reflecting on my options, I realised how grateful I was to have chosen maths as one of my A-level subjects. It became my guiding light, leading me toward a new path: accounting and finance. Financial security had always been an important factor in my career considerations, and this field aligned perfectly with my priorities.

Shine

For the first time in a long time, I felt a sense of excitement rather than obligation.

Looking back, that last-minute change was one of the best decisions I ever made. Had I forced myself to continue with dentistry, I know I would have been miserable. The greatest lesson I have learned is to listen to my intuition. Had I listened to my gut sooner, I might have saved myself from all that unnecessary stress and self-doubt. In the end, I truly believe everything worked out for the best. Sometimes, we become so fixated on the idea that there is only one path to success that we fail to consider whether a better path exists. Life is not about cutting corners; it is about enjoying the journey and being open to change. There is more than one way to reach your goals, and sometimes, taking a different route is the best decision you can make.

With that mindset, I stepped into university, eager for a fresh start. The first day of university was a whirlwind of emotions. Excitement buzzed through me at the thought of a fresh start, a new beginning filled with endless possibilities. But alongside that excitement was a lingering sense of apprehension. Navigating the sprawling campus with its maze of buildings, endless hallways, and lecture halls tucked away in unexpected corners was nothing short of overwhelming. Finding the right room at the right time felt like a mission, and I quickly realised that simply following the crowd didn't always lead me to where I needed to be. Despite the initial chaos, it was only a matter of time before I settled into a routine. Once I cracked the bus timetables and figured out the quickest routes between classes, everything started to fall into place. The campus, which once felt like a puzzle, soon became familiar. And with that familiarity came a sense of confidence.

During this period of transition, I had a personal tutor meeting that truly helped me navigate my emotions and uncertainty about my career direction. Speaking openly about my concerns and fears, my tutor provided reassurance and guidance that I desperately needed. They helped me break down my thoughts, reminding me that changing paths was common among many and a step toward finding the right fit. At that moment, I felt seen and understood. Together, we mapped out possible next steps, including the skills I should focus on developing and the opportunities I could explore within accounting and finance. That meeting was a turning point, giving me the clarity and confidence I needed to be able to move forward with purpose.

I am extremely privileged to have lecturers who are not only passionate but true experts in their field. Their guidance and first-hand experience helped make learning engaging and gave me a glimpse into the world of accounting and finance beyond textbooks and tasks. They bring real-world insights into the classroom, often sharing personal experiences from their careers, which makes the subject matter more relatable and inspiring. Their willingness to support students, whether through pre-arranged or informal discussions, has been invaluable in helping me deepen my understanding and develop my critical thinking skills. More than that, the university itself has provided so many opportunities for me to immerse myself in my chosen career path: through guest lectures, competitions, and events hosted by different societies.

One of the most exciting experiences so far has been taking part in a global sustainability finance competition. As part of a team of three, we analysed a company's current sustainability practices and developed innovative strategies to help them improve. It was both challenging and rewarding, pushing me to think critically and apply what I had learned in real-world scenarios. The moment we found out we had been selected to represent our university was surreal. I felt an overwhelming sense of pride, excitement, and just a touch of nerves; knowing that this was a big opportunity, one that could shape my future in ways I hadn't even imagined.

That experience not only strengthened my analytical skills but also made me reflect on my professional development. I realised that to make the most of future opportunities, I needed to refine how I presented myself to potential employers. I started with the online resources my university provided to refresh my CV. They were useful, but I wanted to be sure my CV was not just being evaluated by machines. I needed real, human feedback. So, I booked an appointment with the employability team on campus. During our session, they not only reviewed my CV but also suggested some great additions of which I hadn't thought. Their advice was genuinely useful, and it got me thinking about my LinkedIn profile. Since I was new to LinkedIn and unsure of what to include, I decided to book another session with them to get some guidance. Taking one step at a time, I was feeling more confident about putting myself out there!

Looking back, the journey from feeling lost on campus to finding my place within my field has been incredible. University has been everything I hoped for and more, challenging yet rewarding, confusing yet thrilling. I have grown both academically and personally, stepping out of my comfort zone to embrace new experiences and opportunities. Each challenge I have faced has only strengthened my determination, making me more resilient and adaptable. The friendships I have formed, the knowledge I have gained, and the skills I have developed have all contributed to shaping me into the person I am today. And if the experience so far is anything to go by, I can't wait to see what the rest of the journey holds.

Spicy Brain
By Emilia Rucinska

Upon receiving my ADHD diagnosis, I was overcome by an overwhelming sense of relief; all this time, I wasn't going crazy, and I wasn't 'lazy' or 'unambitious' like many had assumed me to be. Quite frankly, I was a victim of my own brain. Throughout my teen years I had many comorbidities such as anxiety and depression, that were part of my unmanaged, undiagnosed neurodivergence. I hope this chapter enlightens those who read it, whether you yourself struggle with ADHD or any mental illness, or you're an employer, educator, or even a friend of someone with these struggles. My aim is to give you an insight into living with what I call a 'spicy brain'. I'm sure many reading this will relate to at least some of my experiences, and I hope some also feel inspired. We all have our struggles, and it isn't our failures that define us, but the lessons we learn from these difficult experiences and how we grow from them.

Ever since I can remember, I have felt different to my peers, like I was operating on an entirely different wavelength. I found it tough connecting with people; social cues got lost on me, I had an unshakeable sense of shame and carried on my back a sack bursting with self-hatred. If you receive enough negative remarks in your life, you begin to internalise them, and they eventually infect the perception you have of yourself. That was my reality; ADHD meant that as each academic year intensified, the less I could keep up and in turn, the less motivation I had. Each aspect of my life influenced the other: my grades were plummeting, and therefore my self-esteem, mental health and social life did so too. Then because I had such low self-worth, and felt I wasn't really seen by those close to me, I lost all sense of drive or ambition to improve at school. It was an inescapable, never-ending cycle, which drained me of any ambition, energy, or hope.

In my English language mock exam in year 11, I was so burnt out and exasperated from simply holding myself together, that I wrote only one paragraph in the exam, proceeded to fall asleep, and came out with a weak grade 1 (solid fail). I was lucky enough to have a teacher who saw my potential and allowed me to take English for A-level, for which I ended up getting a B grade. I learnt then that, although a little cliche, there always is a light at the end of the tunnel. When sixth form rolled round, the novelty of a new environment, new subjects and teachers, had me temporarily wired on a positive high. I felt motivated, raring to go with a fresh start. I remember how much I enjoyed biology and carried that enthusiasm on my smile walking into each lesson. One day at the start of year 12, my teacher pulled me aside after class and told me that I should really look at my classmates, and realise this isn't the subject for me, suggesting I wasn't as smart or capable as my peers. I'd never felt a punch to the throat quite like this one. Soon enough, I spiraled back into that old, self-loathing state of mind. It wasn't until the middle of year 13, amidst preparing for A-levels, that I got my ADHD diagnosis. It all had become clear: I was impulsive, left things to the last minute, couldn't focus, and experienced mood swings, amongst other horrid symptoms, which impacted my confidence, social life and academic performance. However, it was so validating to know there wasn't anything innately wrong with me.

That first year at university was bittersweet; it was simultaneously the best and worst year of my life. Soon after moving into my accommodation, I was inundated with angry eviction notices and threats from debt collectors. I didn't receive any money from student finance until much later in the year, so I had no money to pay for accommodation, university fees, or to spend on day-to-day necessities. I was living off £40 a week from my parents, who fortunately did what they could to support me, though I could rarely afford a full weekly food shop on top of other expenses. For most of the year, I wasn't able to get a job to support myself. On top of my financial disarray, was my unfortunate living situation; I really didn't get on with my flat mates, and living with them only exacerbated the misery I was already experiencing each time I checked my bank account. The people around me made me anxious, my financial situation made me anxious, and this perpetual dysregulated state completely threw me off my academic game. I missed deadline dates and submitted assignments last minute after pulling all-nighters to get them done, all because I just couldn't balance my studies alongside my mess of a life. I got an email at the end of that academic year informing me that I would have to repeat it. I wasn't surprised, but nevertheless I was disappointed. Had I faced less adversity in my personal life throughout that year, I probably would've passed with flying colours. No ADHD medication could have pulled me out of that rut, but the realisation of having failed a year awakened something within me. I wasn't going to let external factors like these ruin my chances of building a future. I still managed to find great friends and had the support of my family if I ever needed it, so I wasn't as isolated and unlucky as I often felt. That awful year was the best one of my life; I matured so much. Many lessons accompanied the moments of hardship, and I know I wouldn't be so self-sufficient and driven today if it wasn't for that year-long flop.

Today, I've been more successful than ever; I've received high percentage marks in the 60's and 70's for many assignments, accompanied by very constructive and positive feedback from my lecturers. All achieved without medication for ADHD; there are a myriad of contributing factors to which I owe my academic improvement, and the restoration of my mental health. Coming to Swansea University entirely changed the trajectory of my life. The lecturers on my journalism, media and communication course were beaming with passion for their subjects. I was so inspired by their outpouring of knowledge and their deeply engaging teaching style. No exams and only essay-based assignments meant I had long time periods to perfect my work. The lecturers were also so supportive and communicative, I felt for the first time in a while that I had the opportunity to really excel, with a brilliant network of academic staff who really wanted me and the rest of my cohort to succeed. The university has also been great at accommodating my ADHD; allowing for extensions or any additional tutoring when needed.

The experiences from my teenage years and first year of university provided me with several valuable lessons that I hope may be beneficial to you as well.

The first is that sometimes it's a question of your environment rather than there being anything wrong with you. Coming to university to an entirely different place, where I have found the most amazing friends, attended brilliant lectures and studied subjects I am truly interested in, has transformed me into the happiest version of myself. Because of my positive experience at university, and newfound happiness, I decided to engage more with my studies and consider my future prospects. I participated in career experience programs through Career Boost, which helped me rebuild my confidence and acquire further work experience to prepare for the future. Now in my third year at university, these last few years have been nothing short of completely exhilarating. Going from a school system to an institution at which you have so much more independence and freedom was the panacea to my unrelenting stress and sense of hopelessness. University gifts you with the opportunity to forge lifelong friendships, discover what truly interests you, and prepares you for adulthood. The question is whether you jump at all the opportunities thrown at you, which I urge you all to do. Connect with your cohort, your lecturers, ask for help if you need it, try new things, and jump into the deep end. Stepping out of your comfort zone is the best thing to do for self-progression. Whether you have ADHD or not, you will fail at times and make mistakes. I advise you to relax into that inevitability. I was so incredibly lucky to find my people in Swansea and enjoy my course. Things aren't perfect, but the good certainly outweighs the bad. Finally, do not let negative remarks define you. Every setback can be a lesson, an incredible opportunity to become an even stronger person. The hard times are the ones in which you learn most about yourself, and once you accept that fact, the mindset shift will completely renew your view on life.

Opening Doors Through Language
By Fahad Mohammad

The classroom buzzed with nervous energy as my turn approached. Standing there in my oversized Year 7 uniform, clutching my notecards with sweaty hands, I waited for my name to be called. Just one year earlier, I could barely string together an English sentence. Now, here I was, about to present to my entire year group. As I walked to the front, memories of my first days in Britain flooded back – the confusion, the frustration, the determination to be understood.

I was ten when my family moved from Italy to the United Kingdom. The excitement of a new adventure quickly gave way to the reality of being a child in a country where I couldn't fully express myself. In Italy, I was more talkative, always ready with a quick joke or a clever comment. But in England, I found myself trapped behind a language barrier, my personality locked away by my limited English vocabulary. The most challenging aspect wasn't just learning new words – it was the constant fear of saying something wrong. I remember trying to tell my teacher I had finished my work but instead saying something that made the whole class laugh. These moments were frequent in those early days, each one a small wound to my confidence. Yet, looking back, they were also the steppingstones of my journey.

What I learnt during those first months in Britain was something no textbook could teach – the power of persistence. While other children played during breaks, I would often sit with my English language books, determined to master this new language. However, I knew this approach would not get me many results, so I decided to join after school clubs and be more social even with my limited English. Slowly but surely, through playground conversations and lunch break chats, English began to feel less foreign. My classmates, far from mocking my attempts, became my unofficial teachers. They would correct my pronunciation with genuine enthusiasm, celebrate when I used a new word correctly, and help me understand the countless idioms that make English such a colourful language.

Then came that pivotal day in Year 7. Our group project presentation loomed before me like a mountain to climb. The night before, I practiced in front of my mirror countless times, my Italian accent slowly giving way to more confident English pronunciation.

When I finally stood before my year group, something magical happened. The words flowed naturally, without the heavy accent that had marked my speech for so long. As I spoke about our project, I saw not confusion but understanding in my peers' eyes. In that moment, I wasn't the Italian kid struggling with English anymore – I was just another student sharing their work. Even though the applause that followed was for our project; for me, it was the sound of acceptance, of overcoming a challenge that had once seemed insurmountable. This experience taught me that with enough determination and support, any barrier could be broken down.

Now, as an economics student at Swansea University, I often reflect on how that early experience shaped my approach to learning and life. The analytical skills I developed while decoding a new language serve me well in understanding complex economic theories. The persistence I learnt as a ten-year-old trying to make friends in a new country helps me tackle challenging coursework and embrace new opportunities. My journey with language has influenced my approach to economics in unexpected ways. Just as I learnt to see patterns in English grammar, I find myself naturally drawn to the patterns in economic data. The patience required to master a new language has given me the resilience needed to work through complicated mathematical models and econometric analyses. At Swansea University, I've continued to push beyond my comfort zone. As a student representative, I used the communication skills I worked so hard to develop to bridge gaps between students and faculty. My experience in customer service at Lloyd's, where clear communication is crucial, has shown me how far I've come from that ten-year-old struggling to express simple needs.

My volunteer work at the mental health helpline at Mind was particularly meaningful given my own experience with communication barriers. I understood firsthand the frustration of not being able to express oneself clearly, which helped me develop a deeper empathy for callers struggling to articulate their feelings. The active listening skills I developed there – waiting five seconds after someone finishes speaking before responding – reminded me of my own journey with language, where patience and understanding were key. Through my roles in various university societies and as a St John's Ambulance volunteer, I've discovered that my early experience with language adaptation gave me a unique advantage. I'm naturally attuned to non-verbal cues and always conscious of making communication as clear and inclusive as possible. These skills have proven invaluable in high-pressure situations where clear communication can make all the difference. Mastering English didn't just help me academically – it became the key that unlocked numerous professional opportunities. After completing my A-levels at Sir George Monoux Sixth Form, my ability to communicate fluently in English opened a door I had only dreamed of: work experience at Lloyd's bank. Standing in the prestigious banking hall, I couldn't help but think back to that ten-year-old boy who once struggled to ask for directions. Now, here I was, confidently interacting with customers and colleagues in one of Britain's most established financial institutions.

The journey hasn't always been smooth, though. During my second year at Swansea University, I faced one of my biggest challenges yet: securing a sandwich year internship. The process was gruelling – countless applications, numerous interviews, and many rejections. The competition was fierce, and at times, I questioned whether I would find the right opportunity. But the resilience I developed during my early days of learning English served me well. Each application was a chance to prove that I could articulate my worth, each interview an opportunity to demonstrate how far I'd come with my communication skills. The persistence paid off. Today, I work as an assistant underwriter at Tokio Marine, a position that demands precise communication and attention to detail. In this role, I use both my technical knowledge from my economics degree and the communication skills I've developed over my journey. It's fascinating to see how my early language struggles have transformed into a strength – the careful attention to words and meanings that I developed while learning English now helps me excel in analysing insurance risks and communicating with clients.

Recently, my journey came full circle when I was invited to give a presentation to fellow Swansea University students about my experience at Tokio Marine. Standing at the front of the lecture hall, I couldn't help but smile at how far I'd come from that nervous Year 7 student giving his first English presentation. This time, I confidently explained the intricacies of the insurance industry, shared insights about Tokio Marine's global operations, and detailed the exciting opportunities available in underwriting. The presentation allowed me to bridge the gap between my university and professional worlds, helping other students envision their own potential careers in insurance. Being able to demystify the insurance industry and showcase Tokio Marine's innovative approach to risk management was especially rewarding.

As I look toward completing my economics degree and building my career in finance, I'm grateful for the challenging start that shaped me. Learning English wasn't just about mastering a new language; it was about developing the resilience, adaptability, and determination that continue to serve me in every aspect of my life. From that nervous ten-year-old Italian student to an assistant underwriter at Tokio Marine, every step has been part of a larger journey. The journey continues, and I'm excited to see where it leads next. After all, if I could go from struggling with basic English to analysing insurance risks at Tokio Marine in my second language, what other barriers might I break through next? As I continue my studies at Swansea University and build my career in finance, I carry with me the knowledge that with enough determination, support, and hard work, any goal is achievable.

To anyone facing similar challenges, whether they're learning a new language, seeking internships, or pushing through academic difficulties, I want to share what I have learnt: what seems like your biggest obstacle today might become your greatest advantage tomorrow. My struggle with English led me to develop skills that now help me thrive in the financial sector. Every rejection in my internship search taught me persistence. Every challenge has been a stepping stone to something greater.

Just Have Faith
By Faith Adebisi

I can't even remember when I developed a passion for blogging, beauty and fashion. I've always been full of ideas and opinions, and I've always been a girly girl. It's always been a part of me. My parents definitely played a big role in this. My mum helped me start my very first blog when I was in primary school and both of my parents always encouraged and praised my creative streak. As a child, I loved watching my mum put on makeup and going shopping with her would be the highlight of my week. I loved creating and interacting with art and I helped design my Year 6 prom dress. My little sister and I would play dress up games, experiment with makeup and play the fashion show game on Movie Star Planet for ages. Almost everything I would consume (TV, YouTube, Instagram, music videos etc.) I would be focused on the makeup, the hair and the clothes. My sister and I would watch fashion and beauty DIY videos and try to follow the instructions to the best of our ability. I always loved watching makeup tutorials and fashion and beauty DIY videos, so I knew for certain that I was passionate about these things, and I knew they were my hobbies. In my

Shine

Year 6 yearbook for my hobbies section I put down, 'art, vlogging, blogging and talking' and when I was asked what my ambitions were, I wrote down 'singer, fashion designer, vlogger, journalist'.

Because of my curiosity, over the years a wide range of career paths have appealed to me. I've wanted to be so many things e.g., teacher, physiotherapist, diplomat, psychologist, midwife. I also sometimes limited myself and didn't like pushing myself to do what I really wanted. I never stuck to the above career choices because I always felt like I just wasn't good at or passionate enough about the subjects required to do these jobs. School was one thing I always struggled with academically, I loved socialising with everyone, but I hated the subjects because I just wasn't good at the subjects that were reinforced as important, like maths and the sciences. Also anything I was interested in outside of school e.g. art and politics I really struggled to dedicate myself to formally learning in school. I limited myself for a long time because I just felt that since primary school, I couldn't grasp what school required of me. But I gradually started realising that I was gifted in so many other areas. I'm great at speaking and uplifting others, I love socializing. I'm extremely creative and imaginative and I am a disciplined individual. Struggling with school created a lot of confusion for me when it came down to picking what I wanted to study at university. I began questioning if I wanted to go to university at all. However, after being pushed by my parents and myself to go, it is no surprise that I'm currently studying Journalism, Media and Communications with a year abroad at Swansea University.

My course at Swansea University, has allowed me to try out things I'm interested in and has helped me understand what I would and wouldn't want to pursue as a career. I've built a portfolio, created a film, made mock campaigns, tried punditry and all in the two years I've been here so far. I'm spending my third year in Germany to study at Mannheim, and I've been blessed to participate in many different opportunities that Swansea University Career Boost offered like iBroadcast, where I got to work with BBC Scrum V presenter, Sean Holley; practicing presenting skills and creating an online social media presence for local Swansea organisations. This experience was incredible for me. I instantly started working with people who I had never met before. We watched our interview videos again in front of everyone and we were given tips on how to improve. Then we started practicing filming and presenting with microphones and interviewed each other which was really enjoyable. We also had to make short clips introducing ourselves. It was so great, and we were able to watch all these clips back and see how much we had improved. Then we got into groups and were tasked with improving the social media presence of a local Swansea organisation over two weeks and creating a presentation of our plans to show to the companies each group worked with, as well as the companies offering internships. During the two weeks we met with the company, we went into their office, visited multiple locations and met some of the people they work with. I learned so much from this time: making content for specific audiences, video making, presenting and working in a group of many different people. I was so happy with this experience and my group won the little competition set up at the beginning of the experience! It was such a great thing to experience in my first year of university. In my second semester of the first year, I did a Creative

Shine

Media Practice module, and I got the opportunity to make a portfolio website for this assignment, I made a TikTok account where I showcased my outfits and hauls for this assignment which helped me understand just how much I love fashion and beauty blogging/journalism. Running this account required me to be persistent and consistently post almost every day. I really enjoyed the assignment, and it made me love my course even more. This year, I've taken part in the 100th Monkey workshop, a one-day course that allowed me to learn about my presentation and interview skills. I have learned and gained so much from all these experiences.

Thanks to my dad, I grew up watching a lot of political films and reading many books. This helped to shape me into someone who cares about what is happening in the world, speaking up for important issues and advocating for others. At university, meeting like-minded people through the encampment for Palestine in April/May 2024 allowed me to be more active in attending protests and talks. My course is also a great forum for these discussions, as a lot of this course links to real world issues. I have always been an informed and passionate person who enjoys discussion, which has landed me in trouble many times, so I really do enjoy having a space to freely learn and discuss more.

Trying out so many things at university has helped me realise more and more what I enjoy doing. I love presenting in front of a camera and I love to write about specific topics. This realisation led me to start my own Tumblr makeup and fashion blog and a YouTube channel, the summer before second year. My blog is centred around black fashion and makeup, and I have gained a lot of traction on it - my most popular post having 1,050 notes (likes and re-blogs). Running that blog has led to me starting my own YouTube channel which I focus on makeup, clothes, hauls, and video essays. I aspire to be a fashion journalist, blogger/creator and I want to specialise in the fashion and beauty industry especially because a lot of black creativity is excluded from fashion and beauty media. I also want to be a presenter, because I can honestly talk about ANYTHING. I love entertainment and I love art, films, politics, sports and how these things pertain to fashion, beauty and culture. I love to ask questions, and I love to share my opinions. Even when it gets me in trouble, I know I'll keep doing it because it's part of who I am, and I feel that it's important to speak up about things. My course at Swansea has also given me so much interesting knowledge about marketing which I have applied to my platforms, and I would love to apply this knowledge to a business in future as well, probably something fashion-related and then maybe later, beauty. I'm not sure yet but stay tuned for that!

My mum is my biggest inspiration when it comes to being ambitious, putting myself out there and believing in myself. She inspired my passion for fashion and beauty, through her own love of sewing which kick-started her business. She brought me to watch her teach sewing classes, and our frequent shopping trips allowed me to appreciate fashion and makeup from a young age. She is also strong-willed, goes after what she wants and is dedicated to achieving her goals. I've always admired her. She went back to university twice to pursue psychology and remains passionate about what she does. She pushes all her children and especially my sister and I - as women - to chase our dreams and stay focused at aiming towards success. She has always encouraged me and given me new ideas. And I am eternally grateful for that. My younger sister and my little brother, who I've shared everything with for as long as I can remember, inspire me as well. We share all our plans, ideas, secrets with each other without judgement and encourage one another; we're each other's biggest cheerleaders.

I feel like God is leading me on the right path now. It's definitely true because I don't like limiting myself anymore. I believe that if I want something then it's meant for me, and if it's meant for me, I will have it! I allow myself to dream big because my parents have always told me to live up to the name Faith.

Smelling of Roses
By Gemma Rees

When I recall my early school years, they were filled with a passion for learning but hindered by an inability to focus combined with limiting self-beliefs. After GCSEs, I made the decision to move schools to study A-levels, which ended up being a chaotic experience and led me to drop out, compounding my feelings of inadequacy and frustration. My only choice was to enter the workforce. Despite a string of varied jobs, as a sous chef, a waitress, an admin assistant, my ambition never waned. Each role underscored resilience and provided life lessons, but there was still a lack of direction.

In truth, most of those jobs were driven more by necessity than passion. With no clear career path in mind, I often felt like I was drifting from one role to the next. I tried to convince myself that these jobs were temporary but deep down, I feared I would never find anything I truly loved. As a cleaner, waking up before dawn to scrub classrooms, I would replay the choices that had led me there, wondering if I had missed my chance at something more. Walking dogs was a welcome break from the grind, but the solitude only amplified my sense of isolation. Working behind bars and in fancy hotels gave me glimpses into other people's lives — students, professionals, and creatives with futures mapped out — while I remained stuck in the same loop, unsure where I belonged.

The turning point came after four years working in admin, feeling unfulfilled. I decided to enroll in university to study a foundation year in Animal Science, with hopes of becoming a veterinary nurse. All it took was a week's work experience in a veterinary practice to quickly realise that, despite my love of animals, I was not strong enough to put an animal to sleep or deal with injured strays coming in. I had no idea what I would do for the work experience that was compulsory for passing the course, but through a stroke of luck, I was introduced to Professor Lewis Francis at Swansea University. Despite my lack of scientific training, he took a chance on me that would change the trajectory of my life, both in terms of self-belief and channeling my ambition. Professor Francis introduced me to a colleague who introduced me to the laboratory environment, which I fell in love with. This then led me to apply to study for a BSc at Swansea University.

Those first years of my studies were transformative, though not without their challenges. I tried my best to work part-time, unwilling to let go of the idea of supporting myself financially. My routine was grueling—I would wake up at 4:00 am to clean in schools before beginning my university classes at 9:00 am, which were online due to the COVID-19 pandemic. At the time, my grades were below average, I was constantly exhausted, and I felt as though my attention was spread thin. The transition from working to being a mature student was more difficult than I had anticipated. At one point, I was even considering terminating my studies…

I found solace in the resources and support networks provided by the university. The Centre for Academic Success became a lifeline, offering workshops on critical skills like reading literature, writing a thesis, and data analysis. I was initially hesitant to ask for help, but I soon realised that these resources were designed for students like me— those willing to learn and grow but unsure how to begin. Through these resources, I learned to navigate the demands of academia more effectively and gained a newfound confidence in my abilities. My course at Swansea University was incredibly varied, covering topics from plants and birds to molecular biology and medicine. At first, I found it difficult to connect with areas like botany and ornithology, as my interests were more aligned with medicine and molecular biology. However, I discovered that even in these less captivating areas, I could find ways to make the work exciting and relevant to me. For example, instead of writing standard essays or lab reports, I put my own twist on the assignments, infusing them with unique perspectives and interpretations that reflected my personal interests. I imagined how these topics might intersect with human health or molecular processes, and that creative approach not only made the work more engaging but also helped my grades improve significantly.

By my second year, I was still finding my footing and decided to take a Year in Industry placement. This decision turned out to be one of the best for my career. Working alongside researchers in a professional setting gave me invaluable insight into the daily routines of research and a deeper understanding of the academic process. It was during this year that I truly began to understand the practical applications of my studies and saw a clearer picture of my future in research.

The staff at Swansea University played a pivotal role in increasing my confidence, especially Dr. Tamsyn Uren-Webster and Dr. Eva Sonnenschein in the biosciences department. Their unwavering support and encouragement had a profound impact on myself and many of my peers. Dr. Uren-Webster's ability to engage in deep scientific discussions with students set her apart. She didn't talk to us like students but rather as fellow scientists, fostering a sense of mutual respect and collaboration. Her feedback was always honest and constructive, pushing me to think critically and refine my scientific approach. Dr. Sonnenschein also had a remarkable way of interacting with students, treating our ideas with the seriousness and respect of a peer while providing insights that broadened our perspectives. Both created an environment where I felt challenged yet supported, which allowed me to grow not just as a student but as a developing scientist. Their belief in my potential and their willingness to push me toward higher standards were transformative.

In my final year, I felt a renewed sense of determination and focus. For the first time, I felt like I belonged. Acknowledging that my second-year grades wouldn't be enough for a first-class degree, I committed to pushing myself harder than ever. By embracing the support available to me and building on the skills I had developed during my placement year, I managed to turn things around. In the summer of 2024, I was awarded my First-Class Bachelor's Degree in Biological Sciences.

Yet, as is often the case, triumph was followed by uncertainty. I knew I wanted to pursue a PhD, but finding the right project proved challenging. My initial application for a promising project was unsuccessful, and though I was devastated, I refused to let the rejection define me. Instead, I channeled my disappointment into determination, persisting in my search until I found a fully funded PhD project that was a perfect fit. This project, a collaboration between Swansea University and a research institute in the U.S., aligned seamlessly with my aspirations and marked the beginning of an exciting new chapter.

Even now, as a PhD student, I continue to utilise the support services provided by the university. Recently, I enrolled in workshops on delivering effective presentations and enhancing analytical comprehension. This experience has reinforced the idea that learning is a lifelong journey, and the most valuable mindset is one that remains open to new knowledge and skills. Seeking help and making use of available resources is not a sign of weakness but a testament to one's dedication to self-improvement. What distinguishes good students from truly great individuals is their resourcefulness and ability to maximise the opportunities within their reach. The willingness to learn and adapt, no matter the stage of life or career, is what ultimately shapes personal and professional growth. The journey of learning never really ends, and those who embrace this philosophy are the ones who thrive and inspire others along the way.

My advice to students is to embrace every resource available to you, ask questions— even the ones you think are 'stupid'—and never hesitate to share your dreams with others. You never know who might be willing to help you achieve them.

My father always told me I could fall into the worst of situations and still come out smelling like roses, and maybe he's right. But I've learned that success is less about luck and more about mindset. If you see setbacks as opportunities to grow and refuse to let them hold you back, everything you work for will eventually fall into place. The journey is rarely straightforward, and there will always be moments of doubt and frustration. However, those moments are what shape us, teaching us to adapt and find strength in our struggles. I've realised that having the courage to ask for help and the determination to keep going, even when the path ahead seems uncertain, is what truly defines success. As I look back on how far I've come, I know that every setback was a stepping stone, guiding me towards a future I once thought was out of reach.

The Journey Before the Destination
By I.O.

For many, the journey matters more than the destination. Looking back on my student years so far, I've come to realise that every challenge, every unexpected change, and every difficult decision has played a role in shaping the person I am becoming. There were moments when I felt lost, unsure of what lay ahead, but each experience has pushed me to grow in ways I never imagined. Whether it was navigating academic pressures, making important career decisions, or overcoming self-doubt, I have come to understand that personal growth is a continuous process. My journey has been one of self-discovery, resilience, and adaptability. Pushing me to embrace uncertainty, step outside my comfort zone, and grow into a more confident and determined individual. Every setback and success have contributed to a broader understanding of my strengths and weaknesses, reinforcing the idea that progress is not always linear, but each step forward, no matter how small, is meaningful.

Through it all, my faith in God has been my anchor. In the moments when I doubted myself or felt overwhelmed, I turned to prayer for reassurance. There have been times when I questioned whether I was on the right path, feeling as if I was moving without clear direction. However, my faith has reminded me that even when I don't have all the answers, I am not alone. Trusting in God's plan has given me the strength to keep going, even when things didn't make sense in the moment. I have learned that faith is not about having everything figured out but about trusting that each experience is part of a bigger picture. It has also played a huge role in shaping my desire to help others. Seeing the impact of kindness, compassion, and faith in my own life has fueled my passion for supporting others in their struggles. This belief in service and encouragement has become a guiding principle in my career aspirations, reinforcing the idea that fulfillment comes not just from personal achievement, but also from lifting others up along the way.

One of the biggest influences in my academic and career journey has been my family. Their unwavering belief in my abilities, resilience, and encouragement to pursue my passions have provided me with a strong foundation. From a young age, they instilled in me the value of perseverance, reminding me that success is not about following a predefined path but about forging one's own while staying true to what brings fulfillment. My family has taught me that challenges are not barriers but steppingstones, and that failures are simply opportunities for growth. Their guidance has been instrumental in shaping my mindset, reminding me to view setbacks as temporary, and to keep pushing forward despite obstacles. Their support has not only encouraged me to dream big but has also reinforced the importance of humility, gratitude, and continuous learning. By watching them navigate their own struggles and triumphs, I have come to appreciate the power of resilience and the impact of a strong support system in achieving one's goals.

University has been a huge part of my growth, and I'm grateful for the support systems that have helped me along the way. Adjusting to university life came with its own set of challenges, from managing coursework to balancing extracurricular activities and personal responsibilities. However, the resources available at my university played a crucial role in easing this transition and helped me develop confidence in my abilities. The services at my university, especially Career Boost, played a major role in building my confidence when applying for internships. From improving my CV to preparing me for interviews, their guidance helped me secure a summer internship that gave me real-world experience of a work-life style. The process of applying for internships was initially daunting, but through their workshops and one-on-one sessions, I gained valuable insights into professional expectations and industry standards. They even kept in touch throughout my internship, making sure everything was going smoothly. Having that kind of support reminded me that success isn't just about talent or intelligence, it's about having the right people to guide and encourage you. These experiences reaffirmed the significance of mentorship and the role that structured support systems play in shaping a student's career trajectory.

My internship experience allowed me to gain organisation and communication skills in a professional setting. The opportunity to contribute to meaningful projects, manage meetings, and liaise with different teams reaffirmed my passion for my chosen career and helping others. Stepping into a corporate environment for the first time was both exciting and intimidating, but it ultimately helped me grow professionally and personally. Through hands-on work, I learned the importance of time management, teamwork, and adaptability. Each task, whether big or small, was a learning experience that enhanced my ability to navigate workplace dynamics. This experience also highlighted the importance of mental health advocacy and similar areas, further solidifying my desire to pursue a career in the sector that improves and contributes to the community. Observing how workplace culture and policies influence employee well-being made me even more committed to finding ways to support individuals in their personal and professional lives. My internship experiences not only provided clarity regarding my career aspirations but also reinforced the importance of fostering inclusive and supportive work environments.

Additionally, my role as a Student Career Ambassador at Swansea University has given me the privilege of assisting other students with their career paths. I have learned the value of peer support, networking, and the impact of mentorship. Being able to guide and reassure students facing uncertainty in their career decisions has been incredibly rewarding. I have seen firsthand how a little encouragement or a piece of well-placed advice can make a huge difference in someone's confidence and decision-making. Similarly, my role as Welfare Officer for a university society has allowed me to foster inclusivity, provide peer support, and advocate for the well-being of students within my community. These roles have taught me that leadership is not about authority but about service. Through organising events, facilitating discussions, and being a point of contact for students who needed support, I have strengthened my communication, problem-solving, and leadership skills. These experiences have enriched my university life beyond academics, teaching me how to balance multiple responsibilities while remaining committed to making a positive impact.

The evolution of my career aspirations has been a journey of self-awareness. When I first started university, I was unsure of the exact path I wanted to take post-graduation, but I knew I wanted to help others, so I settled on psychology. However, through internships, work placements, and mentoring sessions, I have gained more insight into my chosen career that aligns with my deep-seated passion for understanding and supporting individuals in their mental health journeys. This process of exploration has been invaluable, as it has allowed me to refine my goals and develop a clearer sense of purpose. It has also taught me that career paths are rarely straightforward; they are often filled with detours and unexpected opportunities. The key is to remain open to learning and adapting, embracing experiences that provide both personal and professional growth.

One of the most valuable skills I have developed through this journey is confidence. Initially, uncertainty created room for doubt, but over time, I have learned that self-assurance is built through experience and exposure. Seeking help from services like Career Boost and engaging in professional environments have taught me that preparation and perseverance lead to growth. Confidence is not about having all the answers but about believing in one's ability to learn and improve. This realization has reshaped my approach to challenges, encouraging me to take initiative and embrace new opportunities with a proactive mindset.

With every obstacle, I've gained a deeper understanding of my strengths and weaknesses. The moments of uncertainty, where I questioned my path and abilities, were just as valuable as my achievements. Transitioning from one career aspiration to another and taking on leadership roles have all forced me to step out of my comfort zone. Each step has taught me that growth is often uncomfortable, but it is in discomfort that we find the strength to push forward. Challenges have become opportunities for reflection and self-improvement, shaping me into a more resilient and adaptable individual.

To students just beginning their career journeys, my advice is simple: this is a journey, not a race. No two paths look the same, and that's okay. It's important to embrace change, seek support when needed, and remain open to new possibilities. University is not just about earning a degree; it is about discovering who you are, what you are passionate about, and how you can contribute to the world. Changing directions or exploring different career options is not a setback; it is a part of the journey. By staying open-minded, proactive, and resilient, students can make the most of their experiences and build a fulfilling future.

Grey Scrubs - Bright Purpose
By James Thomas-Wood

When I was six, I proudly declared that I wanted to be a zookeeper. Rather than laughing the comment off or steering me toward something more conventional, my parents simply said, "If that's what you want to do, you can do it." And just like that, my future was set. I would dedicate my life to zoology, forming an unbreakable bond with an Okapi.

Of course, reality had other plans. My career as an Okapi whisperer never quite took off; as I grew up in military communities across different countries, my interests shifted. I was constantly adapting - to new cultures, environments, and challenges. Living among British Army and civilian medical officers, I saw firsthand the skill and charisma of those who served. But it wasn't until I shadowed doctors in a Brunei hospital when I was a little older that something truly clicked. I watched as these doctors built trust with their patients in mere moments, forming a connection that felt effortless yet deeply profound. It wasn't just about medicine; it was about people. Seeing that, I knew I wanted to experience that same connection in my own career.

People often ask why I chose medicine, and it's a question I've thought deeply about. I didn't have a dramatic epiphany or come from a family of doctors, but I've always been fascinated by the human body and drawn to helping people. Medicine offers an endless journey of learning and personal growth. A journey that has become my passion.

Perhaps the practical aspects played a role, but not in the way you might think. Wearing scrubs to work should be a perk, yet somehow, out of all colours, I ended up in grey, the least inspiring choice. Still, that pales in comparison to the thrill of uncovering the complexities of human anatomy and applying that knowledge to patient care. I love figuring out how things work; like why you can't bend your pinky without bending your ring finger (it's due to shared flexor muscles, in case you're wondering). Medicine lets me explore these intricacies while making a tangible difference in people's lives; something no dull set of scrubs could ever diminish.

One of the most defining moments of my medical training was my first encounter with a cadaver. My colleague and I had exchanged nervous jokes beforehand, but the moment we stepped inside, the gravity of it all hit. And, like a true rookie, I made the classic mistake of breathing through my nose. Formaldehyde has a way of lingering, not just in the air, but in your clothes, your hair, your very soul.

Seeing a cadaver bridges the gap between theory and reality. Where textbooks make anatomy seem uniform, real bodies reveal infinite variation. Hippocrates spoke of treating each patient as an individual, and Aristotle suggested that people possess their own unique virtues and abilities. This isn't just true of personality, it's true of anatomy as well. Each person has their own structure, their own uniqueness, inside and out. Understanding this has shaped my approach to medicine. Treatments work differently for different people, and each patient wants to be cared for in their own way. That experience built my emotional resilience and deepened my respect for who we are; not just as patients, but as individuals with thoughts, fears, and ambitions. Each cadaver was once a living person, and that is a humbling thought.

Medical School has completely reshaped how I learn. It's not just about memorising endless facts, it's about adapting, problem-solving, and applying knowledge in real time. The sheer volume of information can be overwhelming, but the challenge is part of what makes it so rewarding. The journey hasn't been smooth sailing, but resilience, curiosity, and a good sense of humour have kept me going.

More than anything, I've realised that medicine isn't a solo endeavour; it's a team sport. Boarding school introduced me to camaraderie, but medical school has reinforced just how vital it is. Being a supportive, compassionate colleague isn't optional; it's essential. Whether it's setting aside differences for the sake of a patient or simply checking in on a struggling peer, these small moments of kindness can have a lasting impact.

Growing up, I saw hospitals as places of healing; safe havens where people went to get better. But stepping into the world of medicine has revealed a more complex reality. Hospitals are centres of care, but they are also environments of risk, uncertainty, and tough decisions. Every day, doctors navigate the fine line between honesty and reassurance, ensuring patients receive the truth while still feeling safe in our hands. Mastering this balance is a skill I'm determined to develop because medicine isn't just about treating illness; it's about earning trust, offering comfort, and guiding patients through some of the most vulnerable moments of their lives.

Swansea University has exceeded every expectation I had. From the moment I first explored my course options, Swansea stood out; but I never could have predicted just how much it would shape my journey. Even navigating my undergraduate years through the challenges of COVID-19, the support I received was unparalleled. The outstanding teaching, the encouraging environment, and the dedication of the staff have all played a crucial role in shaping me into the doctor I'm becoming.

One of the standout aspects of Swansea University is the unique approach to medical education that emphasises patient centred care, clinical reasoning and communication skills. The dedication shown by tutors teaching the Integrated Clinical Method (ICM) is exceptional. Their passion for shaping us into competent, compassionate doctors is evident in every session. Whether it's staying behind after class to go over a tricky clinical skill or sharing the first-hand practical advice you won't find in textbooks, their commitment never wavers. They don't just teach us how to pass exams; they equip us with the confidence and real-world skills needed to navigate patient care effectively. Their enthusiasm is infectious, and their mentorship and guidance has been invaluable in helping me to grow into the doctor I aspire to be.

The anatomy team, in particular, deepened my love for the subject. I've always been fascinated by the human body but having educators who make learning fun and interactive has been a game-changer. Their expertise and passion, combined with state-of-the-art resources, has made this journey truly special. Bedside teaching has also been invaluable; learning from doctors who genuinely care about making us the best clinicians we can be is a privilege. They give us their time, and in medicine, that is one of the greatest gifts a mentor can offer.

Beyond academics, Swansea's support services have been outstanding. Having a personal tutor who is famous on YouTube is a unique experience, but more than that, it speaks to the calibre of mentorship available here. Swansea hasn't just shaped me as a future doctor; it has influenced my personal growth in ways I never could have imagined.

As I inch closer to wielding a scalpel, I find my aspirations evolving. Surgery has always been a dream; the theatre environment, the precision, the exhilaration of a successful procedure. I love the idea of fixing problems with my hands, physically intervening to restore function and change lives. I believe I could become a great surgeon, and I feel deeply I want to be one. At the same time, emergency medicine fascinates me. You need to think fast, act decisively, and perform under pressure and these skills are what I want to refine. I want to reach a point where reacting quickly and effectively becomes second nature, where I control the adrenaline instead of letting it control me. I also love the variety and the broad spectrum of medicine you become exposed to.

It's difficult to decide, but I know I have time. I'm reflecting on every experience, keeping my mind open to other specialties. I've also developed a deep appreciation for neonatology and obstetrics and gynaecology. The beauty of medicine is that it offers endless possibilities, and I'm excited to see where I land.

Medicine is challenging, humbling, and inspiring. Every day, billions of people experience life in different ways, and as doctors, we have the privilege of walking alongside them in their most vulnerable moments. It's a journey I am endlessly grateful to be on, and one I know I'll never stop learning from.

If I could offer one piece of advice, it would be this: don't let anyone make you feel like you're not good enough to be here. When the going gets tough, don't hold back on seeking out support from family, trusted friends and appropriate support services. Medical School isn't about being the smartest, it's about growing into a compassionate, competent doctor. Every student's journey is unique, and those experiences shape the kind of doctor they become. Keep going, because life gets in the way sometimes. Keep your vision alive and believe in yourself.

From Misfit to Success
By Kat Adamczyk-Rees

Being a mature, foreign-settled mum of two girls is not always easy. Deciding on a career change at the age of almost forty seems like a ludicrous step. Combine this with a move and a marriage breakdown and you have a recipe for a disaster…. Or do you?

I have always been good at languages, so becoming an English language teacher felt like the right choice for me. To make it more meaningful, I moved to London straight after graduating from a university in Poland. Teaching felt relentless, so I changed to an NHS position a few years later and felt much more content. A decade on, one marriage, two children, five jobs and seven moves later, I found myself exhausted, lonely, hopeless and depressed. Deciding that a change was the only thing left, we moved once more, to this randomly picked place near the sea called Swansea, to find a new purpose.

I had planned to become a midwife, however, it turned out it wasn't meant to be, as by complete luck, during the University open day, I stumbled upon a group of osteopaths and they turned my world upside-down there and then. I found myself drawn to the idea of moving the body to help it heal naturally. After a lot of uncertainty around funding the degree and being able to do it on my own with two young children, I secured a place on the course and started with no clue what it was going to look like as I had never even seen an osteopath before then.

I had been warned it is an intense programme, but I've made it through so far. I am now in my fourth year of the osteopathy degree. I really thought this was going to be the time where I make these famous life-long university friendships, but I quickly realised that it was easier said than done. I therefore decided to become the group rep in year one, to be noticed among the cohort and heard by the staff and fellow students. I then managed to get the post of university rep in one of the biggest professional bodies that represent osteopaths and have real input in shaping the future of the profession and education in this field, as well as the recognition and a sponsored participation in many national gatherings of this 'small professional world'. Now in my final year, I'm engaged closer with the Student Union and secured the post of the school rep to work with my colleagues and tutors, to influence the programmes taught and make positive changes in areas that really concern all of us. I am also a member of the Beekeeping Society, tending to our first beehive on campus, having an excuse to wear the incredible bee suit, taking time out of the coursework to refocus on my place in nature. Also, with the daunting thought of being a graduate soon and the need to engage with the work market, I have been working with the Swansea Employability Academy and the Enterprise

Team alongside the Research, Engagement and Innovation Services; both teams offered their invaluable support through tailored sessions, expert advice concerning personal and business development, industry trial days and business spaces. However, possibly most importantly, with the help from the Enterprise Team, I was able to successfully pitch my business idea and secured financial support and mentorship, which are now seeing me through to establishing myself as an entrepreneur, too. This was the single most exhilarating moment of my university experience so far, and I am really grateful I got this opportunity.

Getting through this degree has been a rollercoaster. From great days where I am managing to be a student, a mum, a wife, a friend and myself; to times where I lose all faith in my abilities, I have immeasurable doubts, feeling of guilt for not being a good parent, forgetting appointments, not making deadlines and neglecting my relationships and self-care. Top it all off with being a total misfit, the only one in my cohort with children and literally twice the age of my university acquaintances; it is a very lonely place to be, fuelling my sense of insecurity and imposter syndrome. However, from navigating all the setbacks, to now be working on rebuilding my marriage, as well as graduating and starting a business, is more than I thought I could achieve. Despite all the heartbreak, today I smile when I think about the future. The university has been very responsive on many levels; from offering emotional support, to offering guidance and grants to get my start-up business started. They have seen me through some rough times with mental health support and signposting, 1-2-1 meetings to discuss my circumstances and needs, tailored input from the subject tutors and my academic mentor, and even some relaxing wellbeing crafts sessions. I could find someone to talk to about anything - coursework, fears about the future, and current family life. I could discuss my development plans and ask for guidance from my tutors and mentors, which shaped how I approach my career and made me take steps to reach my target clients before I finish my degree, so that things are in place when I graduate. Their invaluable input made my time at university more satisfying, they made me a more focused student, a skilled professional, a developing entrepreneur and an almost-accomplished woman. I would like to thank each and every one of them, as well as my beautiful family. I need to remind myself, though, that nobody did it for me; it was a joint effort.

I think I like being a meaningful part of things, however, most often it does not just happen to me; I need to create these opportunities and then take them. I am a firm believer that studying a subject will provide the basis of knowledge and safe practice. The education gained in the lecture room, however, is only the beginning, which became transparent through various mentoring sessions and during work placement, that were arranged by the university at my request. These were fundamental in seeing beyond the graduation point, which is difficult when you don't know what to expect. There are so many aspects of being an autonomous practitioner, many decisions to make, many resources needed, many forms to complete; and that is all before you even start your own business. Having sincere conversations with friendly graduates, shadowing in local practices and getting expert brand development advice makes me eagerly anticipate the date when I am standing on my own two feet. It also makes me want to contribute back to those who will come after me with similar questions and doubts, to inform and inspire.

I wish to ask *you* today to look at yourself with a kinder eye and with a new sense of understanding, that the university experience does not have to conform to any preconceptions, and it is, essentially, what you make it to be. This is the time to develop future interests, experiment and push boundaries, earn the respect of your tutors, network and establish professional connections, reinvent yourself, regardless of the age you might be or the background you come from, and work on the skills that you identify in your mentors and role-models. The skills I developed throughout my time here are strongly industry-related, as those whom I see are often vulnerable and in pain. *Empathy* must be at the top spot when pursuing a caring career, and without it we might as well be robots. *Listening* skills are invaluable when I am trying to help my patients, and I might be the only person who they feel they can confide in. *Candour*, as I am only human and also a student, therefore can't get things right all the time. And *confidence*, in myself, in the skills I developed, and in the fact that I will succeed and one day become a colleague to all my current role models and mentors.

The bottom line of this chapter is that life throws us lifelines, we just have to take them. Being a misfit is challenging, but it has also facilitated courage, pushed me forward to places I would not have gotten to otherwise. Regardless of all the parties and friendships I have missed out on, I feel that this time has been amazing and possibly made even more valuable by engaging in student life differently to most of my cohort. I may not feel confident about graduating so soon, but I made sure I used every possibility to plan ahead, prepare, and still remain true to my priorities. The message to you is to try to make this experience your own. Ask for help, look for perks, stand out in what you are good at and sometimes work out of your comfort zone. If people don't notice you, find a way to be visible to those who count. Be on committees, get involved with the student union or the reps, venture outside of the university walls, get volunteering, get published (!), work on your business before you leave university, and above all, *do not go through it all quietly*!

I Can't Have it All (I'm Still Gonna Try)
By Lewys Tectonic

'Something is wrong with you. You're different than us. You're not natural.'

Everywhere I've ever gone, those words have been shouted in my face or murmured behind my back. I know when I'm unwanted, even if I can't pinpoint what made me unwanted in the first place. I was just being myself. Isn't that what everyone tells you to do?

I'm getting ahead of myself though. Let's start with the basics.

I'm Lewys Tectonic, 23 years old, autistic and non-binary using they/them pronouns. At 14, I was the first openly asexual and trans person in Ystradgynlais. I was the kid of the activist Olivia* who took me on protests and helped me send letters to Powys council when I was 13. Even when Olivia* stopped fighting, I remained outspoken about human rights and equality, whether it was at protests during 'Pride', or to my teachers and the popular kids at school.

Safe to say, I was public enemy number one. I was used to it, so I just

Shine

smiled as if being called an alien didn't hurt and kept the blinds closed so no one would see or hear me cry. I wrote out my feelings to survive, creating imaginary friends to save me from my loneliness and at home we lived in a world where magic was real, love was welcomed, and bigotry wasn't tolerated.

In the summer between my sixth form years, I went to Swansea and Carmarthen Universities as part of the 'Reaching Wider' summer university program. For two weeks I was living a student life, reading books on Celtic mythology in the library whenever I wasn't working on my assignments or attending the social events the team arranged.

Considering where I came from, I never thought I could be a university student. Walking away with a 74% on my assignment and a trophy on graduation day proved otherwise.

I signed up for a childcare course in Ammanford Coleg Sir Gar, getting work experience in a primary school. Until the pandemic cut that experience short.

To keep myself sane in a house that was slowly driving me insane, I entered the New Welsh Writing Awards 2020. It's a writing competition where you write a prose piece with a Welsh theme or setting between 5,000-30,000 words. I heard about it two months before the deadline, but I still gave it a shot despite having never written a novella before. I wasn't an honorable mention, but the fact that I'd finished my work and put myself out there was good enough for me.

Shine

Then one night my whole world changed. On October 8th, 2020, four years of abuse and neglect got too much, and I ran away from that haunted house to save my soul.

I was lost at sea in a lifeboat.

Homeless for a month, then shoved into supported living and expected to lose all hope for an independent life, I lived with tenants who were one bad day away from institutionalisation and nurses who had no idea how to get me out.

Luckily, I found 'Good Vibes', an LGBT+ youth group for 11–25-year-old based in YMCA Swansea. They gave me the courage and resources to apply to Swansea University.

And in September 2022, I became a student two years after dropping out of college, barely signing up in time for the last slots in the dorms.

University was a harsh adjustment for me, even at foundation year. I supported the staff during the UCU strikes in 2022, getting up at 6am to hold signs I'd painted. I put every effort I could into my modules, which worked since I achieved first class grading in five out of six.

The summer after this my main lecturer in the foundation year asked me to help him with a project. Wanting to bring his research on 19th century prosthetic users out of academia and into casual settings, he decided to make a boardgame inspired by his work. He asked me to consult on the project as an autistic person. For the first time ever, what made me so different from everyone else, was a strength to others not just me.

Subsequently I was made an intern on the project. I mostly took detailed minutes during the meeting which I then had to convert into less detailed summary notes. Along with that, I shared my insights and opinions about directions the project could go. After months of testing different equipment and unique solutions to the accessibility conundrum; 'Legless in London' was born.

Between the meetings for 'Legless in London', I also spoke with 'Career Boost'. I had some mentoring sessions with a fiction and poetry writer who spoke with me about how to enter the creative writing industry. 'Career Boost' also set me up for work experience days with the Dylan Thomas Centre and Swansea Museum. I only had one day at each location, so I made it count.

The Dylan Thomas Centre was a perfect location as far as work environments go. I loved the peaceful but informative and curious atmosphere. I was really interested in the ability to adapt to different roles throughout the day, whether it was cleaning the display cases or working as a receptionist. Swansea Museum was similarly peaceful and curious, with the bonus of getting to organise some of the donations the museum received. Thanks to my busy summer, I learned more about the types of work environments I like. I already knew that I liked helping people, but now I knew how I could do that. Data entry at the museum helps people who care about preservation find what they need. Receptionist work at the centre helps people find information about things they care about. I'm not sure what field I'll go into in the future, but I know I like small teams where there's always new tasks to do or the chance to talk to people if I'm sick of screens.

Shine

I didn't think my first year could be as busy as my foundation year, but I was wrong.

I was successful in my second attempt to become a student ambassador. During 'Open Days' it's my job to welcome guests to the university, point them in the right direction and tell them why they should come to Swansea. This is a really important role, and the staff asked me to help with the Foundation Year stand. For anyone who thinks they don't have what it takes to be a Uni student, this is the place where they can see that there's always another way.

There was one last part of the 'Legless in London' project I still had to do, even if I wouldn't be paid for it; playtesting. To make sure the game was ready for market, I had to organise lots of meetings so lots of different people could try the boardgame and suggest improvements for it. Thanks to that, it's now available for pre-sale on the official website.

Then the 'Ambitious About Autism' program helped me secure a one-month internship with the DVSA as a digital content designer for July 2024. My first week I was a little shy and kept to myself, as I'd never worked at a real job before, nor was I used to being the youngest person in the room. Slowly though with playtests and treats (because who doesn't love homemade marshmallows), and the support of my line manager's line manager, I opened up to my coworkers, and even got invited to a birthday party.

While at the DVSA, I learned how to edit the intranet pages and the importance of writing in plain English, a new skill for a flowery writer such as myself. I had to manage competing interests from a formal style guide and people who wanted the pages to have a friendly tone, sometimes spending an hour discussing the wording of a single sentence. I'd never managed that sort of working environment before, and I was really surprised when my line manager asked me to stay for another month.

Now that I'm a second-year student, I don't know what's next. But I do know that I'm going to live my life to the fullest, never back down from what I want and never let anyone decide where I deserve to be.

I spent so many years of my life hiding and never taking chances because I thought wherever I went, I would be unwanted. But it's only through the vulnerability of putting yourself out there, as authentically and honestly as you can, that you find the places that will open their doors to you and people who will cheer you on as you walk through those doors.

I'm still learning how to love myself and help people, while chasing my dreams of being an activist and a writer. I'm learning how to ask for help and be my dysfunctional self.

The path may be thorny, but that's expected by now.

*Names have been changed.

Every Twist and Turn
By Lily Carline

'What do you want to be when you grow up?'

It's the question you hear from friends, parents, and teachers throughout your early life; one that some seem to be born knowing the answer to. For me, it was a much messier journey—a collage of big ideas, self-discovery, and a healthy dose of trial and error. Looking back, I've never been one of those people who knew exactly what they wanted to be when they grew up. In fact, I might be a case study in career indecision. But perhaps that's where the beauty lies; in my crooked, flexuous path to finding a meaningful occupation.

For much of my childhood and adolescence, I was a proficient musician, studying flute at a conservatoire throughout my GCSEs and A-Levels. Music seemed like an obvious choice, and perhaps the only one I ever thought I'd do —a ready-made career path rooted in years of dedication. But at some point, I realised that I didn't want to do it professionally. The passion I had for music felt incompatible with the pressures of making it a career. When I let go of that option, I was left floundering. What next?

With no clear answers, I opted to study psychology at university. It felt like a logical choice, one that aligned with my empathetic personality. From a young age, I'd shown a natural aptitude for caring for others, particularly, other children with special educational needs and disabilities. Psychology seemed like an extension of those qualities, a way to channel my compassion and curiosity about people into something meaningful. But as my studies progressed, I became increasingly disillusioned with the career prospects for psychology graduates. The job market was saturated, the routes to my ideal roles were long and convoluted, and frankly, it felt like a dead end for me.

That's when I decided to pivot towards a bachelor's degree in healthcare science, specifically, cardiac physiology. It was a bold switch, but one that felt exciting and right for me. Throughout my year studying psychology, I toyed with the idea of a more patient-facing role, and cardiac physiology offered a structured, diverse career that aligned perfectly with my strengths and, crucially, my ADHD. I am eternally grateful to the course admissions tutor at Swansea University for giving me the opportunity to interview for the course, despite me not hailing from a traditional science-based educational background. The variety in the role promised to keep my mind engaged, while the clear goals and pathways for progression provided a sense of direction I'd been missing. For the first time, I felt like I had found a field that could sustain both my ambitions and my attention.

Once I had joined the cardiology cohort at Swansea, I promised myself that I would begin putting myself out into the professional world, something I would have found more difficult with my first degree. Going the extra mile, as well as discovering what was out there alongside my BSc, became a top priority for me. Subsequently, clinical placements, networking events and mentoring played pivotal roles in shaping my confidence and perspective. There's something transformative about being thrown into high-pressure environments with diverse personalities and professions. You learn quickly how to adapt, how to read a room, and how to keep your composure when it feels like everything is about to fall apart. Each placement added another layer to my professional armour, helping me navigate situations that would once have left me paralysed with self-doubt.

Mentorship, too, has been invaluable. While many people I encountered during my academic and professional journey were helpful in their different ways, one person stands out: Beryl Mansel, my tutor from Swansea University's 'Leadership Academy'. She was instrumental in encouraging me to step outside the confines of academic study and embrace extracurricular opportunities that allowed me to develop 'big ideas'; ideas I didn't even know I had. I signed up for the 'Leadership Academy', with the promise I made to myself at the forefront of my mind: putting myself out there, discovering what was beyond my degree curriculum, not realising it would be a pivotally positive moment in my academic and professional prospects. Her guidance helped me to trust in my potential, to see beyond the next assignment or exam and think instead about the broader opportunities available to us as healthcare professionals, on regional, national and international stages; research, policy and public health. It's a rare gift, finding someone who sees you not just as you are, but as you could be.

Thanks to Beryl, I was inspired to begin attending events and applying for programmes on a national level, further extending my perspective of this profession and others. During my time attending these events, I have met some of the most outstanding, motivated individuals and been totally inspired by their grit and seemingly endless work ethic. I attended conferences, networking events and even a national programme dedicated to fostering leadership skills for healthcare students - the future of healthcare. Thanks to this programme, run by the Council of Deans of Health, I met colleagues hailing from all corners of the UK, bringing their varied and sometimes incredibly niche professions with them. I had the privilege of listening to their own paths, how they discovered their professions, and the challenges they faced along the way. In turn, my faith in myself and my choices grew, as I felt I had been shown how far I could take my profession; the sky was the limit. They helped me see that a career journey is unpredictable and non-linear, to not limit myself and always take any opportunities that may arise, even if they fall outside of the bounds of my chosen specialty; experience and skills are always transferable.

Reflecting on the skills I've found most valuable in my career development so far; it's tempting to rattle off a list of technical competencies and industry keywords! But the truth is, the soft skills have mattered just as much, if not more. Adaptability stands out as a clear winner. The ability to pivot, to remain flexible and open to new opportunities, has been a lifeline in navigating my career path.

Emotional intelligence too, has been essential: the art of reading people, building rapport, and maintaining empathy even in high-stress situations. These are the skills that don't necessarily show up on a CV, but they are the glue that holds me together.

If I've learned anything about careers over the years, it's that perspectives change. When I first started university, I thought of work primarily as a means to an end: financial independence, stability, a sense of purpose. But as I've grown, so too has my understanding of what a career can and should be. It's no longer just about ticking boxes or climbing a ladder. It's about finding joy in the process, about learning what energises you and leaning into that. The emotional maturity that comes with age has been a game-changer. As an 18-year-old, it's easy to see everything in black-and-white terms: success or failure, progress or stagnation. But with experience, you realise that there's so much nuance, so much grey area, and that's where the real growth happens.

So, what advice would I give to students just beginning their career journey? First and foremost, embrace the uncertainty. It's easy to feel like you need to have everything figured out from the start, but the reality is that most people are making it up as they go along. And that's okay. The important thing is to stay curious, to keep exploring until you find what lights you up. Don't be afraid to pivot if something isn't working. Careers are rarely linear, and some of the best opportunities come from unexpected detours. Secondly, invest in relationships. Find mentors who inspire you, colleagues who challenge you, and friends who support you. No one succeeds in isolation, and the people you surround yourself with can make all the difference. Listen to their advice, but don't be afraid to chart your own course. After all, it's your life, not theirs.

Finally, don't underestimate the power of resilience. There will be setbacks, disappointments, and moments when it feels like the universe is conspiring against you. But those moments are temporary. What matters is how you respond to them. Pick yourself up, learn from the experience, and keep moving forward. As cliché as it sounds, failure is often the best teacher.

In hindsight, I wouldn't trade my winding path for a straighter one. Every twist and turn has taught me something valuable, whether it was about the wider world, my career, or myself. And while I still don't have all the answers, I've come to realise that maybe that's the point. A career isn't a destination; it's a journey. And the best journeys are rarely the ones you plan to the letter. They're the ones that surprise you, challenge you, and ultimately, transform you. So, here's to the uncertainty, the resilience, and the joy of figuring it out as you go.

Everyone Moves at Their Own Pace (And That's Okay.)
By Mia Bergin

I was quite young when I was diagnosed with Autism and ADHD, but it took me ages to get the right support at school as I felt like I was walking around as a label and not a person for a while. I felt I was such a problem when all I wanted to do was just sit down and focus but the stress of just being in a classroom with a large number of students made me zone out and doodle because that's all I felt I could do. Going to school with anxiety is like something is out of place all the time and that makes you start to panic. The worst part about it is you know there is no reason to be panicking about how the ceiling isn't symmetrical or how someone's pen sounds, but when you realise this, you start to think the thing that is so out of place is you.

I think I'll start by saying that during school, university was not something I would have put in the top 20 of my bucket list. It's very clear that something I did struggle with, with a taste of self-doubt, was over thinking.

If you had asked me a few years ago I wouldn't believe I was going to university (mainly due to my struggles at school). In college I felt very well supported through my time there and with the right adjustments in place I was happy. When the time came to apply to universities, I was excited and really wanted to go. I am very sporty and knew Swansea was good for surfing which made me want to go even more.

Just before I was due to start at Swansea University, I was very anxious, but the university provided great support by hosting an induction for students with ASD. At first, I was nervous to go but the experience allowed me to familiarise myself with my surroundings by taking a tour around the city and campus. I also met some great friends who were also into the same sports as me, and we are still friends now.

The first month of university felt the longest, I didn't realise how much I would need to do by myself. Even the most basic tasks took me ages to do. It took me 3 weeks to start unpacking my clothes. This isn't because I was being lazy, I knew I wanted to stay at university but in my brain, this felt like the task that committed me to it, like a point of no return. I got to a point where this one task of unpacking became so overwhelming I struggled to get out of bed and even answer my emails. I felt under water like I was being held down by a small task which was slowly suffocating me. To overcome this, I arranged a meeting and spoke to the ASD team who were welcoming and provided me with some great techniques to help me settle in. Part of the advice which really helped me was to do something I enjoy so I went surfing. I wouldn't say it magically solved my problems, but it reminded me that I liked being here. My advice would be when anything is building up no matter how small or urgent the matter is, do something you enjoy.

Progressing through my time at university I thought a lot about joining societies, but I didn't have much confidence, especially in big groups of people. When I'm in large groups of people or even surrounded by unfamiliar people I go bright red and feel like the world is closing in on me and all I can do is ask myself why? I know now that due to my anxiety it's more about managing it then trying to solve it.

Fortunately, I made a friend in one of my classes who invited me to go along to a snowboarding session. I knew about the club through Freshers' Fair, which is an event where you can meet all the different societies. It was something I knew I would enjoy and over time I have made some good like-minded friends. I hope you as the reader can find the courage to experience new things even when they are scary so you can gain the ability to answer your own questions and challenge yourself, because that's what matters. There are still times when I get waves of anxiety but it's okay because I am around a good group of people. So, try something new, you don't have to be the best at it, and you can try lots of different societies and find what makes you feel comfortable with yourself.

The end of year exams come round much quicker than you realise and it's easy to get caught up with everything going on in your life. I struggled a lot with procrastination and found it hard to stay focused, but I spoke with my mentors and there are lots of different techniques and apps to help you get through it. Exam season can cause you to start questioning yourself which is often accompanied by stress.

The university has lots of support options and I contacted the academic success team, which is open to all students, where you can arrange one to one support meetings to help manage your time and workload.

It's not uncommon to find yourself bringing up life's bigger questions. For example, what do I really want to do in the future? Is all this stress even worth it? These questions can be scary, especially when you feel uncertain about what you want to do. I have learned that it's perfectly okay not to have all the answers right now (which I know sounds a bit cliché) but I'm still figuring out what I want to do in the long term, and I want you, the reader, to know, that it's completely fine. What's important is recognising the effort you put in now has value, beyond just the grades you achieve.

Whilst at university I thought a lot about my career journey and through researching I decided to get a part time job within the student union, when I felt ready. It helped me to build on my confidence by talking to a range of different people who I would normally not have contact with. I also contacted the career team which has allowed me to find placements on hospital wards to help me gain a better idea of what I would like to do in the future. It has allowed me to experience different fields of work I would not normally have access to and opened my eyes to the choices I have available. During my career journey I have realised the skills you develop, the resilience you build, and the personal growth you experience are what matters and it's okay if you are unsure.

Reflecting on my journey, I now know that I am interested in cardiology and hope to go on to studying it further after my time at

Shine

Swansea. If I could give any advice to myself at the start of university, it would be to engage as much as I can with my lectures and not get upset if I am struggling because there is support available. It can seem like a lot of reaching out for support, or in my case even admitting you need support, but once you make the first steps, life does get better. University can be a scary experience, especially when you're dealing with a lot of different emotions, but it's also an opportunity for growth. Every challenge, from unpacking that first box to facing a difficult exam, is a step toward becoming more resilient. I've learned to take things one day at a time, focusing on what I can control and letting go of what I can't. This mindset has helped me navigate academic pressures and social aspects of university. Support systems are there for a reason, and you shouldn't feel anxious using them or worry about what other people think. They have really helped me to find a direction for the future and I am excited to see where studying cardiology will take me. Surrounding yourself with people who understand and support you makes a world of difference. Whether it's friends or mentors, these connections can provide a sense of belonging. I realise that the journey is less about reaching a specific destination and more about the experiences and lessons you gather along the way. So, be kind to yourself, take things at your own pace, and remember that your university experience is uniquely yours and everyone will struggle at some point. I have written this chapter hoping that some people can relate to it and find comfort in knowing things don't always go the way you plan them, but you will work through it, even when you think the whole world is against you.

Lots of Lucky Little Detours
By Oluwatosin Alatise

Whenever someone new asks about my university experience, they realise the years don't quite add up - I always smile and say, 'Oh, I just took the scenic route.' Then we both chuckle, the ice breaks, and we move on to something much more interesting.

What I've come to see is that; in one dismissive sentence, I reduce years of hard work with incredible highs and serious lows to a joke. Despite that dramatic tone, this doesn't particularly bother me. I like telling jokes to make people comfortable, particularly at my own expense.

The years leading up to university were really tough. I was born and raised in London and attended a well-known, independent school that frequently sent students to Oxbridge. I was fortunate enough to never think of university as unattainable but rather an expected, necessary step in my undecided career. As a result, I romanticised university greatly before applying.

I started at Swansea University in September 2020, six months after the

UK's first lockdown. However, I'd been housebound for two years before this, starting at the beginning of Year 13 (September 2018), stuck in a lockdown of my own. I never really recovered from that illness and my final grades didn't reflect how I had ended Year 12 – with lots of promise. Despite being in and out of hospital, I managed to pass three interviews to receive five offers for uni. But, on results day I was awarded CDD for all my efforts. I came to Swansea through clearing, and thankfully, they offered a second chance to achieve the academic expectations my family had set for me as a young, 'gifted' child.

It is strange to admit that coming to Swansea University was never the plan, but even the best made plans can go awry. It has been a great experience; shaped by the friends I've made, nights by the sea and a realisation that I may have ended up where I needed to be.

I chose to study Materials Science and Engineering, a subject most people have never heard of, that is offered at fifteen universities at undergrad nationwide. Luckily, Swansea University is one of those institutions. The city's proximity to Tata Steel (RIP – Port Talbot's blast furnace) meant that, in 1920, the demand for further research in metallurgy (study of metals) spearheaded the establishment of Swansea University. I was a fresher as Swansea University celebrated their centenary, but this was considered a rough time for first years everywhere. For me, while unconventional, I still managed to have a good time. Although, I know this wasn't the case for everyone on Bay Campus. Listening to lectures online and watching experimental labs instead of doing them wasn't ideal but having a beach by your accommodation and the wellbeing support from the university made a huge difference.

Unfortunately, after achieving a 1st class average in first year, the problems that began in sixth form followed me to university. This led me down the scenic route I mentioned earlier. Though, I was determined not to let it stop me in my tracks, as it almost had before. Despite persevering to attend university initially, the stakes of this disruption felt higher. There were so many consequences, so when I chose to defer second year, I didn't take it lightly; it would be worthwhile.

Now, I had nearly a year at my disposal, how was I going to spend it?

Well, at the start of second year, I had added a year in industry to gain relevant experience. I had applied (late into application season) to three renowned companies. One got back to me, inviting me to an assessment centre, days after I'd decided to defer. I declined, explaining my situation then hung up to ceremoniously scream into my pillow. Mourning an opportunity I'd forgotten I'd applied for, and the year I would waste. Not knowing if anyone would even answer, I called the number back. The friendly voice that I talked to before picked up, so I nervously asked if they had any opportunities available. There was, and I somehow (having only completed first year) met the requirements. After Christmas, I passed the interview; the job was mine. If I accepted and moved up north, I would be a Production Maintenance Digital Intern at Bentley Motors.

The first month was lonely, I was the only girl in the maintenance department, the only intern and the youngest by a decade. Eventually, I made friends my age, with apprentices, graduates and placement students. The experience was different to anything I'd ever done before or will probably do again. Regretfully, I wasn't working with luxury cars, and frankly I didn't try hard enough to, but casually seeing Bentleys being fitted together before my eyes was insane. The production line was easily the most impressive, complex process I'd ever seen. The grandeur of the factory, however, didn't match my living situation or the forgotten town it was in. I came to realise many of my colleagues commuted from much nicer northern cities, which made my mind up - that job location would be a dealbreaker. Hands down, the highlight of my time at Bentley, was showing my parents around the factory at a family event. Joint runners-up would be presenting my research project to the innovation team and my week at the metrology department. Overall, it was a great insight into manufacturing, a taste of what a graduate scheme could be like, and a productive break somewhere new.

The return to education was daunting, it would essentially be the first time that I had in-person lectures and labs. I would be with a new cohort. I had to go back to a place, and a mindset, that I hadn't been in for the best part of a year. Even with that pressure, my coursework went well. Then exam season came around and, as it turns out, not having in-person exams since GCSEs (six years ago at this point!) does not bode well. That year, I deferred nearly half of my exams. Then, the anxiety that stopped me the first-time round, overwhelmed me wholly in August resits. Over summer, I was interning at Swansea's Steels and

Metals Institute. It gave me reassurance; that I could apply my degree content and that I enjoyed jobs associated with materials. There was a kind, supportive environment there, everyone would happily answer my questions or show me their current projects. I was even offered help for my dissertation in the coming year.

That didn't work out. Months after the internship, Swansea gave me a fourth chance and I had to decide whether to repeat the whole year or just those tricky modules. And so, in the hopes that I could improve overall, and not be capped at 40%, I chose to do everything again. And to my credit, my grades improved in almost every module. Though, the year wasn't without its theatrics. I cut it fairly close having to do some exams in August as I had every year at Swansea. However, that relief came with the burden of no tuition loan, and sadly the setbacks year-on-year were starting to take a toll. Other students I'd tell in passing would make jokes or ask prying questions and there were also important people in my life doubting whether this was for me.

Ever the optimist, it clicked that, as a second year, I was still eligible for most summer placements. So, I took this opportunity to get a better understanding of what career I wanted because constantly worrying about falling ill and failing a very expensive, disrupted degree doesn't allow you to think that far ahead. Somehow, I secured summer research internships at both the University of Oxford and the University of Cambridge. I chose to spend the summer in Oxford; living in graduate accommodation at New College (where some Harry Potter scenes were filmed), punting on the river (or trying to), studying in the Radcliffe Camera and importantly, carrying out cutting edge research in the department of materials.

At long last, my third and (fingers crossed) final year could begin. Like many before me, I had a dissertation to put off until the last minute. I had graduate roles to be rejected from. And crucially, I was due approximately five mental breakdowns. At the same time, I suppose I also have my last couple nights out on Wind St, last few road trips to Rhossili Bay and a goal to reach as many waterfalls as I can find in South Wales. And of course, my last lectures with the best department in Swansea (no offence to Swansea staff who don't teach materials).

There was a point when I never thought I'd get close to this finish line, one that most people take for granted. It feels like so many people seamlessly get into university, get their degree then a job related to that degree.

For now, I'm trying to graduate; after that, I have no idea. I'm considering the options; working abroad, pursuing further education or switching to something completely different to what I've spent the last five years qualifying in. I'm open to any opportunities as the job market for graduates has become super competitive. I'm not too worried though. There's something to take away from the scenic route, which is that there isn't just one way to get somewhere. Those detours or a complete redirection can lead you to exactly where you need to be, and if it doesn't, you can always turn around.

Follow Your Dreams
By Sarah Howell

Coming from an average working-class family and growing up in the 1970s and 80s, the roles of male and female were set in the stereotypes of the time. Typically, with hard working men supporting their families and hard-working women staying home to bring up the children and take care of the home. Education, I believe, was seen as no more than a necessity, something that all children must do; going to university was never in our vocabulary as a family. I did, however, have dreams of what I wanted to be when I grew up. I also had a strong desire to travel and an acute need to help when I saw the news stories on television. Disappointingly none of these desires developed beyond being the dreams of a child. I completed my school education with a few GCSEs and went on to attend college, studying Art and Design, the only thing I thought I was any good at and with no clear vision of where it might take me. On leaving college, I entered the world of work, where I remained for 13 years.

At age 30 I became a mother to my beautiful son; I grew up and matured in that instant. My path from then on was set for me. What I wanted to do with my life, what I wanted to be, were not questions that I asked myself anymore. I was a mother. I was filled with a love, a desire to protect and a clear path that I had never experienced before. My son was born with a lifelong health condition that required surgeries, medication and frequent hospital stays and checks. This very much cemented my role as his mother and carer, nothing else mattered. I soon became a single mother, which although difficult in many ways, I loved and continue to be very proud of.

When my son was two and a half and just four months after his life saving surgery, I returned to work. Along with the need to financially support the both of us, I was, I think, seeking an identity beyond that of a mother. I was lucky enough to gain employment throughout my son's childhood that suited our needs at certain times, working day shifts that suited school hours, and then when he was older, working term time in a school, enabling me to spend the holidays with him. I am aware that not every parent has this luxury and how lucky I was in finding this sort of employment.

It was while working in the school that my health deteriorated, in that I developed osteoarthritis and the frequent pain and discomfort affected my mental health, something I had already battled with on and off for years. I had also entered perimenopause which came with its own issues, brain fog and memory problems to name just two of many. I was starting to struggle to carry out my role at the school, things were becoming problematic. Ever the problem solver, I realised I needed to find a solution; while job searching something more suitable, I had a conversation with a neighbour who of similar age had started university. I decided then that I was going to educate myself and train for a job more suited to my new personal situation. As I did not meet the requirements to go straight to university, I needed to complete a level 3 qualification first. I was influenced by my niece, now a qualified nurse who had recently completed an Access to Nursing and Health Professions course prior to attending university. I decided to follow the same access course. Within two weeks I had enrolled, reduced my working hours to part time and made the necessary financial arrangements for benefits and funding to help support me while I was studying. It was equally a nerve racking and exciting time.

I found studying on quite an intense course after over 25 years out of education challenging and it took some time to adjust to deadlines, researching, writing, and revising. Being in my late forties and with symptoms of perimenopause adding to the challenges, I often wondered if this was the right time for me to study. Despite my initial doubts, it was the right time. I had more time for myself with my son turning sixteen and becoming more independent, going into sixth form himself. We were both studying on level 3 courses at the same time. From the start of the course, I enjoyed learning again and realised I wanted to continue in education as long as possible. A part of the access course was assisting us with university applications and in four short months of starting, at age 46, I had applied for a place at university. I completed the access course with grades I am proud of which earned me a place at university to study Psychology and Counselling.

Shine

In September 2022 I resigned from my job to study full time. Another nerve-racking time, especially financially as a single income household, but worth the risk to fully commit to my education and hopefully improve my life and widen the scope of employment opportunities in the future. I completed the first year of this course but although I very much enjoyed it and found aspects of it very interesting, I decided it wasn't the right fit for me, and I started to look at alternatives. I then applied through clearing to Swansea University's BSc Health and Social Care course. Within a few weeks of starting this course I knew it was more suited to my needs and interests. The modules were as broad and varied as the health and social care sector is. I found this variety kept my interest, and the modules were relatable and some topics I had a personal understanding of.

Since starting my studies at Swansea university, I have found my confidence increasing. In part due to the good grades I have obtained but also from the validation and support I have received from lecturers, my mentor and university support services. My personal tutor and academic mentor, Denise Thyer, has been of tremendous support throughout some very difficult times this past year, and is a fountain of knowledge on anything I ask. We share similarities in life's challenges and circumstances and in seeing how her career has panned out due to the work she has put in, I have really found her inspirational, to the point of considering following the path of lecturing as a career.

When beginning my studies I had, and still have, a strong desire to be self-employed. I would like to start a business or a social enterprise, as there is, I believe, more possibility of creating a career that suits my needs and interests. I am intending to seek help in this endeavour from the university student enterprise department in my next semester. I have, however, considered other careers since studying health and social care and discovering the vast employment opportunities there are in these fields. While recently co-hosting a new university podcast called Health and Social Care Heroes, an opportunity that became available through and alongside Doctor Sara Jones the programme director and Simeon an employability expert at the university; I met and interviewed such inspiring people who have various careers in health and social care. Hearing their stories has opened up possibilities in areas of the sector that I was not previously aware of.

The decision to become a student in my late forties took some consideration, as a single parent I needed to think about how the changes to our homelife and structure might affect my son. Would I be able to manage financially? Would I even be capable of studying on a degree course? What if it did not work out? I spent time considering each of these questions and decided it was something I really wanted for myself, so much so that I would make it work. I am so glad I took this opportunity, being now in my 4th year overall of returning to education. I am enjoying learning, and I am excited for what the future might bring. I have already had experiences and taken opportunities that would never have even entered my thoughts before. In some ways I feel I have come full circle back to my childhood dreams and after a lifetime of helping wherever I am able, I am now on my way to developing my desire to help in a profession that will hopefully see me through the rest of my working life.

Shine

If you find yourself considering university and in a similar situation to me, a parent, a potential mature student, or experiencing any other barriers to education, I will say do your research so that you are informed but ultimately go for it! There is so much support available to help you through your studies, be that financial, professional, employment or personal support. I truly hope you find inspiration to follow your dreams too.

Dreams vs Reality
By Siân Gibson

For the longest time, I've known my dream. I can't count how many times I was told it wasn't realistic. But what does realistic mean anyway?

People's perceptions of me have become my definition. My thought process was, 'how do I change their perspectives of me?' and not 'why should I change myself to cater to them?'

I thought my dreams were impossible, not achievable, just a figment of my imagination. But the word itself states I'm possible.
So, what is actually stopping me?
The real answer, the biggest answer, was limiting beliefs.

I guess you could say I was a smart kid. Unfortunately, smart isn't exactly synonymous with being fulfilled. Being academically inclined made me more self-aware, emotionally. And that, in itself, became crippling. Sometimes, putting other peoples' needs before your own becomes second nature. I wanted to be reliable, I wanted people to trust me, but it seemed that being self-aware would cause more issues for me. Establishing friendships had to go two ways. Being at school always made me feel dreadfully uncomfortable, because I couldn't be authentic. I felt like I had eyes at the back of my head 24/7. The insecurity mainly came from my skin, but also lack of confidence in myself. I was the embodiment of insecurity, because I made myself lack authenticity. I lacked the ability to have artistic expression, which is what truly made me happy. My insecurities, being put on a pedestal for my academic achievements, caused an extreme fear of failure in what I actually wanted.

I soon realised that there was little point in establishing friendships if I couldn't be myself and establish a genuine connection with others. It seems this was one of the many reasons I developed hyper independence. Being alone became a coping mechanism, and somehow, it still is.

The emotional roller coaster would settle itself once I reached college. College was a happy place for me. I felt free. I felt like I could truly express and become the person I wanted to be. But I gave into the voice in my head that I still couldn't do music. That I had no previous experience, that it wouldn't get me a job etc. I gave up opportunities to learn because I thought I wasn't good enough. The limiting beliefs came forward again. The limitations other people had put onto me. Whether it was the easiest option, or it was because I was afraid of failure, I don't know. But academics seemed the easiest way out, because I was still interested in the topics I was studying, until I learned an extreme lesson: that I am not my academic output.

That might have been the hardest lesson to learn. I thought I had failed, pretty much, in life, after I got those grades. I put so much expectation on myself to get a certain grade, to excel in all my subjects at college. I realised, through stopping myself having the artistic skills I truly desired, through stopping myself actually performing, I was creating a strain in other areas of my life. I felt like I was forcing myself to be someone else, to repress what I truly wanted, in order to fit into how others viewed me.

My sister has always been an inspiration to me, perhaps in a daunting way. I never told her enough that I admired her work ethic. Some of the things she achieved still don't seem humanly possible to me. I think what stuck out to me the most is her ability to be so confident in what she wanted to do. She was adamant that she knew what she wanted to do, and that nothing would stop her. She let her own opinions dictate her success. I want to thank her for that. I want to thank my family for the person they've allowed me to become. My parents are, funnily enough, like my best friends. Being around my parents is like being swaddled in a comfort blanket. If I could wish for anything from them, it would be to have more time with them. Sometimes, I just wish they knew that life isn't always about achieving something every day. I'm tremendously grateful that they are starting to come around to that lesson. I sincerely adore my parents, and I wish to do nothing but to make them proud. Even if I didn't get as much time as I ever wanted with them when I was young, I can feel that starting to change.

Due to the way I'd grown up, being alone led to me realising music felt like the only way for me to feel. Music regulated my emotions; music consoled all my emotional pain; performing gave me euphoria because I felt seen. Music exists solely to tell a story. It doesn't criticise the person who told the story, or comment on that person.

Instead, it highlights a story in itself.

In all honesty, I think my love of music came from a distinct grief or loss, whether that had been people who had passed on or people I've loved that I had to walk away from. However, I'm grateful for the loss of those connections. Without it, I would never have known that music and performance are part of my authentic self, even if I've repressed it for such a long period of time.

Coming to Swansea University would definitely be something I have counted as an adventure. The prospect of it at 18 years old felt terrifying; moving country, being hours away from home, learning how to live alone etc., but coming to this University has potentially been the best experience of my life. Career wise, I've had the opportunity to explore development of my own company, work in mentoring for language in schools, and pursue the legal field. Personally, I've had the opportunity to learn, to grow, by living alone. Through studying at university, it started to highlight that I have a lot of interests in different career paths through going to open days etc. I was luckily enough to work with MFL Mentoring through university, which allowed me to realise that I enjoy teaching. By attending career fairs, I was able to look into work as an academic teaching assistant, as well as work with Reaching Wider; an organisation which shows the benefit of higher education to young children.

In terms of mentorship, my academic mentors have definitely helped my professional development. Cerys, my first academic mentor, was the first lecturer I met at an open day in Swansea in 2021. She had a very nurturing way of helping me, particularly in my first year when I had to go to hospital, and I'm forever thankful for that. When academics became too overwhelming, my current academic mentor - Victoria - helped me. On top of this, I feel very fortunate to be allowed to study a dissertation in music law, where my passion lies. My dissertation lead has definitely helped me grow and develop in this area.

As well as this, Swansea University allowed me to connect to Career Boost, and Jade, who has helped me more than she will ever know. Career Boost has not only enabled me this opportunity but has also given me a business grant in order to allow my business to trade. As well as this, Career Boost has helped me progress my book launch by connecting me to TG Consulting, as well as brilliant publishers. These are two major goals, specifically in the creative arts, that I have always dreamed of completing. Alongside this, I had the opportunity to visit South Korea, somewhere I have dreamed of visiting since 15, through Swansea University's Go Global experience. Studying in Korea had its ups and downs; going to hospital, then going into my speaking exam straight afterwards, but it left me with some incredible friends and memories. I'm sincerely grateful for this experience. The connections and friends I have made from going to this university have helped me to realise who I actually want to become. I want to thank them all personally for that. Now to be going into my third year, I realise attending this university feels like rediscovering myself, and who I aspire to become.

As much as I originally wanted to go into Law, I know my heart is in music. Whether that is in the legal side, or in the creative side, is something I still need to figure out. Going to university has definitely helped me develop lyrically, as I'm no longer as afraid to write.

Sometimes, I do find academia to be overwhelming, but through doing academics, I can now pursue my calling with the knowledge of how to protect myself legally whilst creating. I now know learning is more important than my output. As long as what I achieve benefits what I actually want to do, and not what others' want for me, there will always be success. My definition of success is what I want to achieve for myself, what I want to be for myself, not what others want me to achieve, or be. I wish I could go back and tell my younger self that everything is possible. All I wish to become, all I wish to achieve, is attainable. I just needed to believe it's attainable.

The little girl who dreamed of being seen, being heard, needing her emotions validated; all these things will always be possible through music.

Breaking Barriers; A Tamil Girl's Journey to the Stars
By Tirzah Velauthapillai

Some journeys begin with a clear path, but mine began with questions: Who am I? Where do I belong? What could I become? Growing up between cultures, across countries, and often feeling like a puzzle piece that didn't quite fit the picture, I still knew I was part of the art. My story isn't just about studying aerospace engineering, it's about breaking barriers, staying rooted in my identity, and proving that no dream is too distant when you have the courage to reach for the stars.

That journey of self-discovery became even more real when life moved me (quite literally) across borders. When I moved from the Netherlands to the UK at the age of ten, it felt like stepping into an entirely new world. The accents were unfamiliar, the customs different, and even the way people interacted was new to me. I often felt like an outsider; lost in translation, both culturally and emotionally. But instead of shrinking under the weight of it all, I saw it as a chance to grow. Each challenge taught me resilience, adaptability, and the value of perspective — qualities that would later shape my path into aerospace engineering. Through all the changes; new homes, new schools, and life's unpredictable twists; two things never wavered: my family and the identity they helped me build. From an early age, my parents rooted me in our Tamil heritage and Christian faith. These weren't just parts of me, they were my foundation. My culture gave me pride, and my faith gave me strength. No matter how unfamiliar the world around me became, I carried something unshakable within me. That sense of self became my compass; grounding me, guiding me, and reminding me that even when everything changes, I still belong.

It was from that place of grounded identity and hard-won resilience that I made one of the boldest decisions of my life; to study aerospace engineering. In many ways, it was a radical choice. It's a field dominated by men, with few women, and even fewer Tamil women. But I was drawn to the stars, to the idea of pushing the boundaries of what we know and what we can achieve. The first time I walked into my lecture, a wave of excitement and uncertainty washed over me. I quickly became aware of how different I was from those around me. In classrooms and social settings, I often stood out, whether in appearance, speech, or perspective. At times, the weight of expectations and stereotypes felt overwhelming. But as I navigated these moments, I made a choice. Instead of blending in, I embraced my uniqueness. I came to understand that my differences were not obstacles but strengths. They shaped my perspective, giving my voice value and making it one worth hearing. As the first person in my family to attend university, let alone study aerospace engineering, this was a monumental achievement. My parents, who moved to the Netherlands due to the civil war in Sri Lanka, had sacrificed so much to give me this opportunity. They didn't fully understand the path I was choosing, but they supported me with all the love they could. For them, and for myself, I was determined to succeed.

One of the most rewarding aspects of my journey is the impact it has on those around me. When I talk about my studies, people are curious, asking questions about the field, what I'm learning, and how it all works. When I tell people what I do, their reactions are often ones of surprise and pride. Their faces light up, and I see the admiration in their eyes. Their excitement is contagious, and I love sharing my passion for aerospace with them. It's a moment that fills me with warmth, knowing that I am not just pursuing my own dreams, but also challenging stereotypes and paving the way for others. These moments remind me that I am not just on this journey for myself. I am also representing my family, my community, and my heritage. People often ask how I manage the challenges of being different in such a demanding field. I tell them that yes, it can be tough, but it's also incredibly rewarding. The differences I meet, whether cultural, gender-based, or otherwise; are opportunities for learning. They challenge me to approach problems from unique angles and uncover solutions others might overlook, ultimately shaping me into a more innovative engineer and a well-rounded person.

Still, for every visible success, there were invisible struggles that often go unseen. Beneath the surface of my journey are moments that remind me how much harder the path can feel when you're carving it alone. I still remember the day I needed to complete a simple DBS check. For most people, it was just a formality; tick a few boxes, get someone to verify it, and move on. But for me, it became an unexpected two-day mental spiral. I sat at my desk, staring at the screen, trying to think of someone I could turn to. A lecturer? A professional contact? A family friend? Nothing came to mind. That moment hit harder than I expected; it wasn't just about a form. It was about realising how alone I felt in navigating this path. While others seemed to have ready-made networks, mentors, or family friends in professional roles, I had to figure things out from scratch. It was a quiet, painful reminder of the unspoken gaps I carried with me as a student; the invisible weight of trying to build a future without the support structures so many take for granted.

But that low point became a turning point, this experience sparked a deeper understanding of the importance of seizing every opportunity. I knew I needed to adopt this mindset if I was going to overcome the hurdles before me. So, I contacted my university team. The support I received from Swansea University was a game-changer in my academic journey. From the very beginning, the university provided a wealth of resources to help students navigate both academic challenges and career development. One of the most valuable services I accessed was the university's Career Services, where I received tailored advice on CV writing, cover letters, and interview preparation. At first, I was unsure how to present my diverse experiences in a way that would appeal to employers in the highly competitive aerospace industry. With the guidance of career advisors, I learned to highlight my skills and unique background with confidence. Workshops and career fairs were equally invaluable, offering the chance to meet industry professionals and better understand what companies look for in graduates. One particularly impactful moment was attending an aerospace-specific career fair, where I connected with representatives from leading organisations. These interactions not only expanded my network but also gave me clearer direction and insight into the vast range of pathways within aerospace engineering. Through the 'Career Boost' program, I was even able to take part in writing this chapter and receive additional support. These experiences were instrumental in building my confidence and preparing me for the real-world application process. Networking events organised by the university and external organisations played a significant role in broadening my professional circle. I made it a point to attend as many as I could, knowing that building a network was essential for future opportunities. Each event became a classroom of its own, teaching me how to communicate effectively, ask meaningful questions, and leave a lasting impression.

I realised that growth doesn't only happen in lecture halls; it happens when you show up, speak up, and take a chance on yourself. During an internship, I worked on cutting-edge technologies, including drones, propellers, and aeroacoustics; areas that are incredibly relevant and exciting today. Looking back, I never would have imagined myself involved in such a groundbreaking project. It taught me the importance of taking risks, applying for opportunities even when they seem beyond reach, because sometimes, the most unexpected steps lead to the most extraordinary experiences. The friendships I formed during my studies were equally transformative. My course mates were more than just peers; they became pillars of support. We tackled assignments together, shared ideas, and motivated each other through the challenges of our studies. Their friendship was a constant reminder that, while I may have lacked initial connections, I was capable of building meaningful relationships that could enrich my academic experience.

So, to anyone reading this who has ever felt like they didn't belong; know this: your difference is your power. Like every star shines in its own way, so do you. Embrace it. Chase your dreams boldly. The path may be unfamiliar, but it's yours. And it's worth every step.

Through the Loops; Resilience in the Face of Life's Roller Coaster
By Therese Elnar

Throughout my childhood, I was raised by my parents and extended family in the Philippines. When I was about 8 years old, my parents made a big decision to emigrate to the UK to be able to provide for my stepbrother and me. This meant we'd be under the care of our grandparents and aunt (who had an incurable illness) and stay in the Philippines. Even with my parents away, life at home seemed to continue as normal.

At the end of March 2014, and the last few days of being a grade eight student my history teacher tasked our class to imitate some WWI images she had pre-selected. My group were given a photo of men in the trenches during the war. Unfortunately, my classmates were the 'nice and popular but actually horrible' type. The photoshoot went well until the end when it became completely sour. It ended with me trapped in a sewer, having to be rescued by my best friend. I was distressed and I cried about this to my parents on the phone and then made a big decision on the spot, 'I'm moving to Britain'. They were quite nervous when I said this because I was distraught, even asking, 'Are you sure you don't need more time to think about this?'. Despite them being anxious about me being firm on such a big decision, I stood my ground and said that everything will be okay. I felt sure that a fresh start was on the horizon for me.

After getting good grades in my GCSEs in 2019, I was lucky to get onto the A-Levels I wanted to sit and the sixth form I wanted to go to. As we all know, the Covid-19 pandemic struck in 2020. This is when my mental health struggles really started to show; depression made me struggle to focus, and relationship and friendship breakdowns had made me paranoid to step outside to get some fresh air. I also got a late diagnosis of Autism after a recommendation to sit an assessment by my support worker at that time, which made me a bit distraught. All these struggles then started to build-up, and I got the news I dreaded the most;

'I'm sorry, but your Year 12 grades are too low to progress and we recommend repeating the year.'

I was completely devastated, and this led me to have numerous mental health episodes. Thankfully, the second time I attempted the academic year, I just scraped by to get into year 13. Unfortunately, another relationship breakdown then led me to not do too well in my A-levels (I was even ill for one of my chemistry papers… jeez) and I got grades that must be every aspiring student's worst nightmare: grades C, D and D. I thought it was the end of the world, and no university would take me in. At this point in time, I thought 'I think this is the end of the line for me.'

I emailed my firm choice and Swansea University about the circumstances I went through during my exam period and I thought they would not excuse the challenges I had faced. However, their reply would change that entire trajectory and my mindset where I thought I would have to leave my dreams behind.

'With the right support…' – 2022. To my surprise, the university accepted me with a condition and an alternative offer. Through UCAS, they said that due to my horrid grades, I had to undertake a foundation year. At first, I was hesitant to take this offer as I was worried about falling behind and losing time. However, the admissions team were helpful; explaining that I could switch to my preferred course after the foundation year; chemical engineering with a year in industry. Additionally, I realised that a foundation year would give me an opportunity to adjust to a completely new environment, which was much needed given that I cannot cope well with big changes in general.

They gave me another option as well during a phone call. I could partake in their Materials Science course instead and go straight to first year. After doing some research, despite some similarities between the courses, I thought that it didn't align with what I wanted to do in the future. Hence, I accepted the offer to take a foundation year. With the options laid out to me, I felt that life at university would benefit me because of how flexible and understanding they were about mitigating circumstances; and I wasn't even a current student at the university yet!

Shine

In the summer of 2022, the university offered a transition event designed to help autistic students adjust not just to Swansea University, but to the city as a whole. However, due to the limited interaction I experienced during the event, I decided not to stay for its entirety. I recognised its value for others, but I preferred to explore the city and university at my own pace, which I did with my boyfriend by my side.

It took the foundation year to adjust to everything: flat mates, a different city, and living on my own. Academically, I didn't need to worry about the foundation year as the majority of the content covered were things I already knew and felt confident in. This was the year I got introduced to my support worker who honestly, if I hadn't had, I know I would've dropped out by now. I also took the opportunity to take part in being a student ambassador for the university; helping during open days and other events the university ran. Eventually, I was able to join their digital content creators team, where I made multiple pieces of content for their social media channels and also took part in marketing photoshoots. It was a good opportunity to make a profit from my hobby, which is videography. It was also a pleasant surprise to find that assisting at open days wasn't like secondary school where you did it for free; instead we were paid an hourly wage.

In January 2023 I had a shocking and unfortunate event occur unexpectedly; my relative who raised me and who had Neurofibromatosis Type 2, had deteriorated fast and passed away. This meant I had to fly home to the Philippines to help with the funeral and any legal things that needed to be carried out. As this was during the January exam period, I had to inform my faculty regarding this and they were really understanding, saying that they had deferred my exams to the summer and this allowed me to head back without worrying about my studies.

If there's one thing I'd take away so far, it would be the fact that the staff at the university are empathetic. I've only told you about the academic side of support they offer, but their wellbeing and disability team are just as good; they made sure that I basically didn't end up dead in a ditch! I honestly have never expected to get this much support from the university.

'My knee!' – 2023. More unfortunate events were to come. One day in September 2023 whilst cycling home, I ended up hitting a pole, falling awkwardly twice and dislocating my kneecap (shoutout to the good Samaritan medicine student who helped me that day; thanks by the way!). This led me to miss Fresher's Week and the majority of my lectures in the first week of my chemical engineering degree. Moreover, an incident in the late autumn left me feeling uneasy about attending university lectures in person. Consequently, I often chose the comfort and security of staying indoors as it meant that I didn't need to go through the hassle of preparing to head out with an immobilised knee.

Socially, I became isolated; no one really visited me during this time other than my boyfriend. I knew absolutely no one on my course other than the lecturers. Academically, I was only able to go to the four lab sessions for one of my modules as it was hard getting around physically.

'Hopefully, this year would be better' - Now, 2025. This chapter is for those who've had a lot of changes in their life: parents working overseas, moving abroad after typical high school drama goes too far, mental health spirals and possibly life-changing discoveries about yourself. I'd want you to know that I hear you and that your experiences are valid. I'm hoping my story would not only inspire you to aim high and persevere through any struggles, but to also, if you're going through some bits that I mention, to reassure you that things will get better despite sitting in the storm currently.

Crohn's University and Me
By Willow Browning

"To my incredible grandparents, there are no words capable of truly expressing my appreciation for you both. Your never-ending love and support has strengthened me to be the person I am today, and this chapter has been a wonderful way of putting it into perspective.

All my love, Willow."

After attaining a first in my dissertation and an overall 2:1, I truly understood the extent of my passion for my degree and the depth of the obstacles I had to persevere against which have made me incredibly proud of my achievement. From this experience, I learned that sometimes taking a risk can be an incredible stepping stone when it comes to deciding our futures. A common phrase that has stuck with me is 'the world is your oyster'. This well-known phrase provided me with a sense of empowerment to pursue my dreams.

When I was deciding on the content of this chapter, I came to understand the significance the concept of 'History' has played throughout my life. There is no part of my personal history more important to me than the pride and inspiration taken from my family. I may have come from a more traditional 'working class' background but my family played a significant part in ensuring the freedom of the world we live in today. My great-grandfather served in the Korean War as part of the 'Glorious Glosters'. They defended South Korea from Chinese invasion alone for several days before capture as Prisoners of War. His father, respectively, served in WW2 at Dunkirk and on the other side of my family, my great-grandmother served in the 'Women's Land Army'. These wonderful people who I am fortunate enough to have as my family, served as my first introduction to history. My education gave me both a sense of what their experiences were like and why their contributions in the name of duty will forever be so significant. However, my enjoyment of history as a subject emerged during my A levels. I learned about the ruthlessness and cruelty of the Nazi regime which contrasted with the Civil Rights Movement in America. My engagement with the latter paved the way for a desire to study history at degree level.

However, sometimes these dreams are paved with their own challenges which are each unique to shaping who we are. I was raised in what some may consider a 'non-traditional' model as I lived with my grandparents from around 13 months old. These circumstances arose due to the severeness of my mother's struggles with Multiple Sclerosis which deteriorated her ability to take care of me. I was born prematurely and faced complications including several major surgeries and permanent blindness in my left eye. My situation was made more stressful with the deterioration in the relationship with my father as a teenager, resulting in our subsequent estrangement as he went on to 'start' a new family and today I have little to no contact with him. At the same time, I was diagnosed with Crohn's disease. It would have been quite understandable for anyone facing such dire challenges to feel isolated and depressed and there were times when I felt no one could ever truly understand what I was going through. Without the support of the rest of my family I would never have felt truly capable of pursuing my dreams.

Yet, this did not deter me, and I enrolled into Swansea University in 2021 to do a bachelor's degree in history. My first year was challenging as I felt isolated within the student halls and overwhelmed with the transition from rural to city life. I also had to balance having medical treatment for my Crohn's which could be draining and at times made me feel separated from my peers. I am fortunate that I made several very close friends which was a huge positive as we did similar but different degree subjects, and I embraced them as they too likely faced some similar insecurities. I really enjoyed the diversity in my modules as I studied both Ancient Greek and Roman societies. One highlight was my essay on King George VI (King Charles III's grandfather) and how his contributions to British History have been overlooked; for which I achieved a first. My second year was a far more positive experience. I moved into a student house which made managing my Crohn's far easier as I had a positive support network around me. I continued modules on Medieval Britain studying the origins of dragons with source material which was incredibly fun and engaging! Yet the depth of my university experience here was not only in my academic work, but the growth I experienced as a student volunteer and project coordinator at Discovery SVS. In this role I took on the responsibility of creating and overseeing the running of activities and events for disabled adults within the local community; a challenge that allowed me to flourish within a supportive and friendly environment.

The personal development I have undergone would not have been possible without the support given to me by the university programmes and staff who helped pave the way for many different opportunities for me. As part of the 'Career Boost' programme, I was eligible for support purchasing work attire to wear at interviews and they helped to arrange a really meaningful and practical short internship for me at Caredig; a housing association group based in Swansea and the surrounding areas. As an intern, I was able to build upon my teamwork skills in a new environment where I had responsibility sorting through outstanding rent arrears but having the impetus placed upon me to be aware of the sensitivities involved and to treat everyone without judgement. Furthermore, it was a very engaging experience to witness their daily operations and to have the chance to both sit in on and contribute to team meetings as I worked my way through my set tasks and was encouraged to speak and comment upon individual cases. Finally, it was fun to collaborate with those on my team and engage in a group quiz for Mental Health Awareness week, an insightful and fun break which in some ways was just as valuable as the practical experience I was gaining! Overall, it was a wonderful and challenging experience, and I would recommend it to anyone as it allowed me to gain experience outside of the university environment. Furthermore, I also had the opportunity throughout the semester to have one on one appointments with a careers advisor where I could dive into job applications and talk through the entire process with them. I could get advice on what to write based on my skills and experience and receive feedback on how to better promote myself. It was also really beneficial as we built up a great working relationship and this helped me with my ideas about a career path. My career ambitions now seemed far less daunting, more achievable and realistic for where I was in my development and where I wanted to be in the future! In terms of my future career goals, I have two main aims. Firstly, I would love to attend and be part of academic conferences promoting my capability at writing to a professional standard. As this is such a competitive field, I aim to develop my writing through getting feedback from my lecturers on my writing style and creativity but to also embrace any opportunities to attend that come my way. Secondly, I desire a career where I can see the difference I can make to someone through providing support and seeing them flourish.

Therefore, I will be looking to utilise my careers advice to navigate employment opportunities that compliment my volunteering experience!

Overall, I feel incredibly proud of myself when reflecting on the last 3 years. I attained my 2:1 while juggling the side effects of my Crohn's; dealing with appointments, completing issued tests, taking my medication and dealing with flare ups in my symptoms whilst still trying to meet deadlines. Witnessing that I overcame this through being organised and embracing my friends, allowed me to ground myself and be able to come up with solutions for any difficulties I was facing. What next? Well, I have begun a Masters in Medieval Studies at Swansea after receiving such positive feedback on my dissertation! The rest of my story is less clear cut but that is ok! I plan to keep working hard at what I love and take up the opportunities that come my way!

Invest in Yourself
By Yasmin Santiago

No one really talks about how much first-year students struggle. While some people seem to be fine and eager to move out, it's okay to feel anxious and sad; just know that you aren't alone in feeling this way. It's a learning curve that all of us have to navigate, but if you push through it, you can really enjoy your time. A new environment doesn't have to be overwhelming. It's full of new experiences and friendships that you can form, and each experience will teach you more about yourself.

Starting university was difficult for me; it was a completely new environment that felt unfamiliar and, quite frankly, overwhelming. Everyone always says that university is the best years of your life, but initially, I didn't believe that. My anxiety was quite bad, but luckily, I made good friends. We all talked about how we felt and helped each other adapt to this new environment. My best advice is to take some time to settle in, try your best to make friends, and go out to explore, even though it might be tempting to stay in your room. It took me a year to adjust to my new life, but once I did, I felt much better and learned how to cope with being away from home. Managing the workload and the newfound freedom was an interesting challenge. The transition from college to university assignments was completely different, and I found it difficult to cope, especially since I had never written 3,000-word assignments before.

Once I settled in, I felt more comfortable putting myself out there and exploring my capabilities. I dedicated my second year to focusing on myself and my career, and it has been the best decision I've ever made. Let me explain why:

I initially wanted to be a writer or journalist when I started university. However, shortly after beginning my course, I changed my mind. I didn't want to limit myself regarding future career options, and I wanted to pursue something I would genuinely enjoy. So, I decided to focus on what I enjoy and see where that takes me.

During one of my modules, I spoke to Dr Sarah Williams about the marketing profession as I was interested in it, and she encouraged me to research more about it and see if it would be something I would be interested in pursuing as a career path. When I was in my second year of university, I decided to take a risk and try something new, so I applied for iBroadcast Media Academy, where you had the opportunity to attend masterclasses with other students and two professionals who would teach you many new skills. iBroadcast Media Academy is an extracurricular activity comprising masterclasses and a project. The project was to complete the social media marketing of a non-profit organisation. We were assigned 'The CAE' and worked as a team to meet the organisation's marketing needs. We then presented this in front of a panel of employers and students. This experience was pivotal in my career journey as it helped me build professional self-confidence, allowing me to take risks and try new things. I was then invited to attend the 'TG Next Gen' talent experience, which allowed me to implement these networking skills. This event allowed me to connect with like-minded individuals and build my network. I went with a good friend of mine who was on my iBroadcast team and we helped each other during the event. It was less intimidating to have someone I knew with me, and we had a nice time.

After iBroadcast, I applied for internships and did digital marketing for 'The Elements Retreat' by Zen Tent Events. This internship was five months long, and I learned a lot. I thoroughly enjoyed working with the amazing team and attended the weekend wellness retreat in June in Candleston Woods in South Wales. At this beautiful retreat I saw the event come to life and the structure of the retreat allowed me to enjoy some of the scheduled workshops. The breathwork workshops were enjoyable, especially EFT, in which we were shown how to manage our anxiety through a technique called tapping. The whole experience was helpful and allowed me to connect with people working as freelancers and creative individuals. It was one of the best things I have ever chosen to do. And I have been offered the internship again for seven months in 2025, starting in January.

The confidence and skills I gained from this internship allowed me to feel confident in my professional abilities. I will start two internships in

January, one with Zen Tent Events and the other with Swansea University's Students Union. I am looking forward to both of these internships, what they will teach me, and how I can grow as a professional doing something I enjoy and am passionate about.

At 'The Elements Retreat', I made connections that allowed me to begin my freelance journey. The biggest challenge has been that the structure is very different from working in a conventional 9-5 role. To overcome this problem, I ensured that when doing my weekly planning, I left considerable time for myself and my social plans. I want my work to fit around my life and not be everything.

Throughout my Elements internship, I was assigned Kelly Quinn as a mentor, and her advice and guidance made me feel comfortable and part of a loving team. Her guidance and attention to detail allowed us to work together wonderfully, and she shared my passion for wanting to work abroad. She is one of my inspirations as she has interests similar to mine and has encouraged me to live abroad and work remotely; showing me that my dreams are possible and achievable.

My career path has changed massively since being at university because I now know what direction I would like to go in and which career path I am interested in, which is massive as I've never really fully known what I wanted to do for work and what I was good at. From the experience gained at university, I am ready to continue to grow and work towards my goals. The skills that I have found the most valuable in my career development have been communication and confidence. The ability to network can massively help your career, as you never know where a conversation could lead you.

I applied to many internships and was not successful until my Elements internship. This isn't uncommon either; most students are rejected many times before they find the role that is right for them. This feeling of rejection can often make you feel bad, but you have to remember that it doesn't last and if you persist, you can find something better for you. You have to pursue the things that make you happy, not what everyone else wants you to do. University is not just about getting a degree; it is also about having time to have your own space and decide what you want to do with your life or find out what you enjoy. It's easy to overthink what will happen when you graduate, but you just need to calm down and enjoy the moment you are in. The more grateful you become, the easier it will be for you to enjoy where you are right now. It's easy to scroll on social media and compare yourself to where everyone else is, but their journey is different to yours. So don't lose hope, follow your dreams and do the things that make you happy and feel fulfilled.

My perspective has changed as you don't have to do the typical jobs or 9-5. You can do things that you enjoy for work. It doesn't have to be boring. And it's okay to try new things, and if you don't want to continue working in a certain field, it's never too late to change paths.

My advice to you reading this, if you are at the beginning of your career journey, is to make a vision board or Pinterest board of goals and what you want to manifest; then put it on your desk so you are encouraged and reminded of what you are working towards every time you work.

You can also do this for personal goals that you want to achieve in your life. Say yes to more opportunities and put yourself out of your comfort zone to grow. Find an internship or extracurricular project to help you gain experience alongside your studies. Don't feel the need to have everything at once; good things take time. Don't overwhelm yourself and find your balance. Improve your networking skills, build your network whilst you are at university, and make the most of what your university offers. Learn how you work best, find what you are good at and enjoy, and use this to help refine your skill set and, most importantly, believe in yourself.

I want to express my heartfelt gratitude to everyone who has supported and encouraged my journey of growth. A special thanks goes to my dad, whose unwavering support and belief in me have inspired me to pursue what truly makes me happy. Your encouragement means the world to me.

About T.G. Consulting

TG Consulting is an independent education consultancy, specialising in employability, student engagement and social mobility.

Our ethos is to **connect, collaborate** and **create**. Breaking down barriers for students, creating opportunities and building confidence. Daily we engage with students like those whose stories are featured in this book.

Our bespoke services include:

Graduate and student employability

Student training and development

Staff training and development

Student Engagement

Embedding employability frameworks and modelling

Graduate outcomes strategy

Careers & Employability strategy

Social Mobility

Racial Equity

Employer engagement alignment

We understand the higher education and student environment well and can provide useful insights into the higher education space including the student journey and recent trends. This will align your campaigns and products, so you have a clear proposition, targeted solution and campaigns.

We offer a range of services from short-term or strategic support to aligning serviced and team structures, so whatever your challenge, drop us a line and we will connect, collaborate, and create.

Info@tgconsultingltd.co.uk

www.tgconsultingltd.co.uk

Find us on Instagram and LinkedIn.

University Resources and Information

University life offers a wealth of opportunities—creating lasting friendships, gaining invaluable experience, earning a high-quality education, and developing skills that set you up for future success. While the transition to university can feel daunting at first, it's important to remember that support is always available. At Swansea University, we are committed to providing a wide range of services designed to help you navigate any challenge and make the most of your academic journey. Whether you need academic assistance, career guidance, or emotional support, our expert team is here to guide you every step of the way.

Our services are student-centred and tailored to meet your individual needs, ensuring that all students, no matter their background or circumstances, have the support they need to succeed. We aim to provide integrated, professional services that offer advice, guidance, and support, empowering you to reach your full potential, both academically and personally. Through our commitment to equality, diversity, and sustainability, we create an environment where students can thrive in every aspect of university life—from pre-application to post-graduation.

Our team provides expert advice and resources for both immediate and long-term challenges, including financial support, mental health guidance, employability services, and inclusive academic assistance. Swansea University is here to ensure that your university experience is both fulfilling and transformative, helping you to achieve your goals and make a meaningful contribution to your community and the world at large.

Key Support Services and Resources:

- **Centre for Academic Success**: Academic skills development, workshops, one-to-one tutorials.
- **Swansea University Libraries and Archives**: Access to high-quality research and study resources.
- **Assistive Technology**: Tools to support students with disabilities and enhance productivity for all.
- **Swansea University Transcription Centre**: Accessible learning resources for print-disabled students.
- **Residential Services**: Accommodation support and advice, including disability-related housing needs.
- **University Health Centre**: NHS medical services tailored to students' needs.
- **Health and Wellbeing Academy:** Affordable services to support physical and mental wellbeing.
- **Student Wellbeing and Disability Service**: Emotional support, adjustments for disabilities and long-term conditions.
- **Mental Health Support**: Access to counselling, digital services (Togetherall), and self-help resources.
- **Career Services**: Job search support, employability coaching, career fairs, and internship opportunities.
- **Student Support Services**: Financial advice, community engagement, and support for personal wellbeing.

- **Swansea Academy of Inclusivity**: Academic and pastoral support to ensure an inclusive student experience.

Helpful Organisations

This book is full of inspirational stories to celebrate the strength of these individuals who have overcome adversity and barriers in their lifetime. The content of this book is not intended to be a substitute for professional advice or treatment. Always seek the advice of a mental health professional or other qualified health practitioner.

Useful resources

Student Minds
https://www.studentminds.org.uk

Childline

*If you are under 19 you can call, email or chat online about any problems you have.

www.childline.org.uk/-getsupport/1-2-1-counsellor-chat/

www.childline.org.uk/get-support/contacting-childline/#BSL-counselling - if you need a British Sign Language interpreter.

www.childline.org.uk/get-support/message-boards/ - message boards to talk to other young people in similar situations.

Phone helpline opening times:

9am - midnight, 365 days a year, 0800 11 11

PAPYRUS

Confidential support for under-35s at risk of suicide and others who are concerned about them. Open daily from 9am–midnight.

HOPELINE 247

0800 068 4141

Shine

88247 (Text)

pat@papyrus-uk.org

papyrus-uk.org

OCD Youth

Youth Support for young people with obsessive-compulsive disorder (OCD).

ocdyouth.org

NHS

NHS app with confidential health advice and support for 16–25-year-olds.

nhsgo.uk

SANE

Charity that offers emotional support and information to anyone affected by mental health through their out of hours support line.

http://www.sane.org.uk

The Mix

13–25-year-olds can receive advice on any problem including discrimination, drugs and money.

Helpline: 0808 808 4994

www.themix.org.uk

Victim Support

If you've been a victim of any crime or have been affected by a crime committed against someone you know, victim support can help you find the strength to deal with what you've been through. Services are free and available to everyone, whether or not the crime has been reported and regardless of when it happened.

Support line: 0808 1689 111.

Stop Hate UK

A confidential 24-hour support service for young people under 18 experiencing or witnessing a Hate Crime.

www.stophateuk.org/call-hate-out/

Boloh

Supports Black, Asian or Minority Ethnic children (11+), young people and parents and carers who have been affected by Covid-19. You can call to talk through any worry or problem. You can speak to someone in English, Gujarati, Urdu, Bengali, French, Spanish, Arabic, Punjabi, Mirpuri, Pothwari, Hinko, Hindi and Sundhi. Interpreters are available for other languages.

Opening times: 10am - 8pm, Monday - Friday; 10am - 3pm on Saturdays and Sundays.

0800 151 2605

Webchat Service: www.helpline.barnardos.org.uk/contact-boloh

Mencap

Information and advice for people with a learning disability, their families and carers. Services include an online community.

0808 808 1111
mencap.org.uk

Scope helpline

Equality for disabled people

https://www.scope.org.uk/helpline/

0808 800 3333 and online support

Diabetes UK Helpline

Shine

0345 123 2399*, Monday to Friday, 9am to 6pm

https://www.diabetes.org.uk/how_we_help/helpline

Sickle Cell Society

Support for those with the condition, including resources for young people

helpline@sicklecellsociety.org

Monday, Tuesday and Wednesday (10am-5pm**)** Valerie – 0780 973 6089

Thursday and Friday (10am-5pm) Sheri – 0208 963 7794

Refuge:

www.refuge.org.uk/get-help-now/for-teenage-girls/

Freephone 24-Hour National Domestic Abuse Helpline: **0808 2000 247**
www.nationaldahelpline.org.uk (access live chat Mon-Fri 3-10pm)

Shelter

Charity working for people in housing need by providing free, independent, expert housing advice.

shelter.org.uk/youngpeople

Young Stonewall

Information and support for all young lesbian, gay, bi and trans people.

0800 050 2020
youngstonewall.org.uk

The Terence Higgins Trust

Growing up and entering the world of sex and relationships can seem confusing and worrying at first. If you are not sure if you are gay, lesbian, bisexual or transgender, you may find it helpful to talk to someone you trust about your feelings. – THT is there to answer your questions and give you some support.

Freephone: 0800 802 1221

www.tht.org.uk

Grief Encounter

Supporting bereaved children and young people.

0808 802 0111, Weekdays 9am-9pm

grieftalk@griefencounter.org.uk

www.griefencounter.org.uk

Children's Society

Help refugees and migrants.

www.childrenssociety.org.uk/what-we-do/our-work/young-refugees-migrants

Red Cross

Different languages to help young refuges aged 15-25.

www.redcross.org.uk/get-help/get-help-as-a-young-refugee-or-asylum-seeker

Help if you are over 25 years old.

www.redcross.org.uk/get-help/get-help-as-a-refugee

Young Roots

A website with help and activities based in Croydon and Brent Cross for Refugees.

www.youngroots.org.uk

Refugee Support Network

http://www.refugeesupportnetwork.org/pages/2-our-services

REAP

http://reap.org.uk/useful-websites-for-refugee-groups/

UNHCR (The UN Refugee Agency)

https://www.unhcr.org/uk/useful-links.html

Gingerbread

Helpline for single mothers and young fathers 0808 802 0925.

www.gingerbread.org.uk

Working families

Information on what you are entitled to at university whilst pregnant.

www.workingfamilies.org.uk/articles/pregnancy-and-maternity-for-students/

Samaritans

Providing emotional support to anyone in emotional distress, struggling to cope or at risk of suicide throughout the United Kingdom and Ireland, often through its telephone helpline.

116 123 (Call)

jo@samaritans.org

Samaritans.org

C.A.L.L. Mental Health Helpline

Offering emotional support and information/literature on Mental Health and related matters to the people of Wales.

0800 132737

call@callhelpline.wales

callhelpline.org.uk

Shine

Adferiad

Provides help and support for people with mental health, addiction, and co-occurring and complex needs, to maximise their personal potential, and achieve a better quality of life.

01792 816600 (South Wales Office)

info@adferiad.org

adferiad.org

www.ingramcontent.com/pod-product-compliance
Lightning Source LLC
Chambersburg PA
CBHW031357040426
42444CB00005B/329